Edward S. Ellis

**The Forest Spy**

A tale of the War of 1812

Edward S. Ellis

**The Forest Spy**
*A tale of the War of 1812*

ISBN/EAN: 9783337299408

Printed in Europe, USA, Canada, Australia, Japan

Cover: Foto ©ninafisch / pixelio.de

More available books at **www.hansebooks.com**

# THE

# FOREST SPY.

## A TALE OF THE WAR OF 1812.

BY EDWARD S. ELLIS,

AUTHOR OF THE FOLLOWING DIME NOVELS:

### RIVAL HUNTERS.
345 THE LONG TRAIL.
347 THE PHANTOM TRAIL.
348 THE APACHE GUIDE.
### ON THE TRAIL.
376 PHANTOM HORSEMAN.
455 THE TRAIL HUNTERS.
460 THE QUAKER SCOUT.
502 RANGERS OF THE MOHAWK.
512 BILL BIDDON.

NEW YORK:
BEADLE AND ADAMS, PUBLISHERS,
98 WILLIAM STREET.

Entered according to Act of Congress, in the year 1861, by
BEADLE AND COMPANY,
In the Clerk's Office of the District Court of the United States for the
Southern District of New York.

# THE FOREST SPY.

"THERE IS A PLEASURE IN THE PATHLESS WOODS."

## CHAPTER I.

### THE SHADOW OF COMING EVENTS.

So the red Indian by Ontario's side,
Nursed hardy on the brindled panther's hide,
As falls his swarthy race, with anguish sees
The white man's cottage rise beneath the trees.
He leaves the shelter of his native wood,
He leaves the murmur of Ohio's flood,
He bends his course where twilight reigns sublime,
O'er forests silent since the birth of time.
SCENES OF INFANCY.

THE night was cloudy rather than dark. The straggling clouds continually sweeping across the moon's face, rendered the light treacherous and uncertain. The vast forest and silent river sometimes blent in one gloomy field, then separated as a flood of rays streamed through the rents in the vapory masses. It was then the Tennessee seemed to collect the light upon its surface, and reflect it with a phosphorescent glow, such as sometimes is seen upon the ocean when the moon is shining without obscuration. The glistening face of the stream was unruffled, only when the plash of some animal along shore set a ring of tiny and widening circles in motion, and gave a tremulous and grotesque reflection of the moon's image, which hitherto had come and gone in the bosom of the river like the figure in the mirror. Now and then the tree-tops were gently bowed by a breath of wind, that wrinkled the river for an instant as it crossed, then sped away through the forest. For miles along shore, tall trees overhung the stream, the branches frequently dipping and resting in the water, and casting a line of shade for several yards from the bank.

Through this obscurity, on an autumn night in 1811, an Indian canoe, containing a single person, was making its way with the most studied caution. The trained ear could have scarcely detected the dip of the paddle, or the occasional brushing of a limb over the shoulders of the man who so silently controlled its movements. At long intervals the frail vessel emerged from the gloom, and glided across the open spaces along the shore, its occupant ceasing his efforts at such times, and suffering his paddle to rest quietly beside, while, without a visible effort, he guided himself onward with the most unerring skill. When momentarily exposed to the gaze of any human eye that might chance to be scanning the river, the orbs of the man flitted with watchful anxiety from right to left, taking in, almost at a single glance, the varied contour of the shore, and every peculiarity of the wood or clearing that came within the scope of vision.

Several times a smile, half playful and half scornful, played around the corners of his mouth. He seemed to be indulging in a reverie as pleasant as it was interesting to himself. He was a man rather spare and tall, of a nervous, muscular build, with a sharp and rather lengthened visage, smooth-shaven and somewhat furrowed by the wrinkles of time. His hair was thin, rather long, and among the locks that escaped his close-fitting coon-skin cap, could be detected a few glistening locks, which seemed only to give additional firmness and decision to the countenance. The eyes were large, lustrous, set closely together, and ever twinkling with that restless, anxious expression, which is an inevitable peculiarity of the man whose years have been spent amid the perils of the wilderness. His attire was similar to the hunting-dress worn by rangers at that day, being made with less regard to beauty than to safety and comfort. There were no gaudy or unusual colors in it, its hue being such as to blend with the autumnal forest, and afford its owner no extra anxiety on account of its contrast with its constant surroundings. The buck-horn haft of a knife rested against his breast, while the blade was sunk beneath the girdle of his hunting-shirt, and a long, beautiful rifle lay in the canoe in front of him, where the owner's hand could be laid upon it in an instant. The man was one whose characteristics were caution, extreme watchfulness, a nervous apprehension, and, withal, a peculiar species of self-confidence that led him upon all manner of dangerous undertakings.

"I see nothing of the varmints," he muttered, as his canoe entered the sheltering band of darkness, after crossing one of the open spaces mentioned. "I see nothing of the varmints, and yet it was in these parts they were said to be gathering. Twas also said their council-fire would be seen from the Tennessee, and my eyes have deceived me for the first time if the winkle of a camp-fire has been crossed by my canoe. No, no; it must be further on."

While thus communing with himself, the measured dip of his paddle continued. He kept close in under the sheltering shadows, and when the openings were reached, sometimes held his canoe stationary, until the moon was more obscured, when it shot forward like a frightened bird and had crossed the exposed spot before the cloud had passed. He did not pause, even when a tremulous cry, like the wail of some lost one, rose on the air, and was heard long afterward, like the lingering sound of the heavily struck bell.

"That was no human voice," he communed. "I've heard the scream before, so like that of a woman lost in the woods. I was deceived only once by it, years ago, when I took it for some female calling to her friends, and give an answer in the hopes of bringing her to me. She did come; but it proved to be a mighty painter, and she flew at me as if I had stole her young. I've the scars of that scrimmage about me yet. Spitfire never did more shooting or better service than she did for me on that same day."

For a half-hour more the man in the canoe held his way, occasionally muttering to himself, and impelling the vessel less rapidly than heretofore, while his eyes carefully ranged the shore, as if in search of some spot which was not entirely unfamiliar to him.

"'Tis three years, come this autumn, that I hunted in these woods, and I should remember that spot where I sat in the forks of that oak, and counted the six war-canoes of the Creeks as they went past. I took a long look, and I recall now how I thought I should know the place if I passed it on a night as dark as a wolf's mouth; but it seems I am at fault, when the moon shows her face in a way that is plainer than I wish. My eyes are good for nothing if yonder ain't the very oak this minute."

As the man spoke, the prow of the canoe overlapped a portion of the shore which was free from the overhanging branches, and became stationary without noise. Rising to his feet and stepping carefully out, he pulled the slight craft a foot or two up on the bank. Then lifting his rifle in his right hand, he trailed it, and, in a crouching position, made his way forward with a speed which, considering the perfect silence that characterized it, was truly astonishing. Once near the tree referred to, he made a rapid circle around it. Approaching its trunk, he spent several minutes in examining the other saplings and trees, so far as the gloom permitted. Seemingly satisfied with the survey, he made his way back to the canoe in the same stealthy manner as he had left it.

"When one makes such a blunder as that, 'tis a certain sign that his years have begun to tell on him. There is a wondrous likeness between the two trees, it is true; but now, when I think, this is not as tall as was the other by a good half dozen feet when it sheltered me three years ago, and it would never do for such a mistake of mine to be known."

The man shook his head as if displeased with himself, and by the time his canoe had progressed several yards further up the stream, its headway was once more slackened, as he seemed to catch, through the almost impenetrable gloom, the shadowy outlines of remembered objects.

"This bush leaning here into the water, seems the same one through which I first seen the top of the Indians' plumes as they passed up-stream. It is surely of the same hight, and I can't be mistaken in the tree this time."

He had hardly ceased speaking, when his canoe touched the land as silently as before. Pulling it up on the bank, he placed the paddle and his rifle side by side, in it. Then, by a quick effort, he lifted the barken structure over his head, as if it had been a mere plaything, and, with long, noiseless strides, made his way deeper into the forest. A walk of a few rods brought him beside a large fallen tree which he hastily surveyed without removing the burden from his shoulder; when, stooping, he slid the canoe within the cavernous hollow of the trunk as dexterously as if it had been carved out for that very purpose. A few rotten chunks were removed from within, and, guided by his sense of feeling, which years of practice had rendered as perfect as that of seeing, he disposed them in a manner that, under the light of day, would seem to have been done by no other hand than that of time. This completed, he carefully shoved the paddle in beside the canoe. Nothing more was done; for to have concealed his property with any more care would have been certain to betray the whole artifice to the eye of any American Indian who might chance to pass that way.

"It has answered the same purpose before, and ought to do it again," he muttered, as he resumed his crouching position, as much from habit as from the occasion which necessitated it. "The eye of the Creek overlooks many a thing that a Seminole or Shawnee would not pass; but Tecumseh might eat his dinner on that log, without suspecting a white man's property was any nearer than the settlements. But here is the oak, and the camp-fire must be near at hand."

He was now underneath the enormous branches of an oak that towered far above its surrounding companions; and, with an air of satisfied assurance, he gazed upward at its vast pyramid of vegetation, for a few minutes, as well as at its less lofty companions that stood thickly around. That no mistake might be made, where it was really impossible for such a thing to occur, he sprung nimbly upward, and catching a limb in one hand, doubled over it, and was among the topmost branches in the twinkling of an eye. Here he spent several minutes in viewing every part of the forest and river, so far as the unstable light of the moon would permit.

"These eyes of mine are worth something yet," he continued, accompanying the expression with a chuckle like the click of a gun-lock. "They done good service through Harmar, St. Clair and Mad Anthony's wars, and now that it is pretty certain Tecumseh is going to raise a muss that'll make considerable trouble afore it's put down, they may do as good service yet. Tecumseh is a wonderful man—a wonderful man," repeated he, dropping his head, as if in a deep reverie; "and it's lucky he was too young to do any thing in the campaign o' '95, or Mad Anthony would have found a worse foe than Little Turtle, Blue Jacket, Black Hoof, and the other scamps, proved themselves to be. I sometimes feel a sort of sorrow for Tecumseh, when I think what big hopes in his breast are going to be upset. He is trying to stir up all the Indians, north, east, west and south for thousands of miles, believing he can sweep every white off the North American continent. Poor fellow! he's an outlandish fool, for he must know there is a man on his trail who will be sure to outwit *him*; he must have heard of—" The man suddenly checked himself, and then resumed in a still lower voice: "No, it don't befit me to boast of my deeds, though I *will* say, when no one but myself can hear it, there are few men of this day who have done more. Twenty years ago, when I was somewhat younger, and started at the sound of the Shawnee yell like a young gal, I boasted of deeds I had done, and that too, I blush to say, when I would sooner run than fight. I have seen too many seasons come and go since then, and have ranged the woods too often to talk of my exploits."

There certainly was a dash of drollery and humor in the man's composition, for, despite the years of apprenticeship, he often checked himself in this manner, and sometimes braved the self-recriminations that were sure to follow, by indulging in his self-glorification until he had exhausted the stock of deeds with which his memory was filled. Underneath that rough exterior, which seemed schooled by the most perfect discipline, and which, in ordinary times, was as calm and unruffled as the silent forest itself, could be detected the signs of an excitability which, on some occasions, would be sure to assume dominion over one who, at other times, held it in such absolute control. In short, he was a droll, humorous, and excitable man, trained and toned down by years of the most rigid severity, and one in whom the "knacks of nature" were so strong that, when stirred by the hand of passion, they would float for an instant to the surface, only to quickly disappear again.

The eyes of this man had wandered over the dark tree-tops for some minutes, when they suddenly settled upon a point to the north of him, and at right angles to the course of the river he had just left. An ordinary observer would have failed to detect any object that could justify the intensity of his gaze; but while his eyes were roving over the wood, they were suddenly arrested by a small point of light which glimmered for an instant among the trees like the twinkling of a fire-fly. Not five minutes were needed to assure him that the light, being stationary, was a small camp-fire, and that its starlike glimmering was caused by the passing to and fro of human forms before it.

"They are all there, and I must make my observations. If a chap feels sort of sorrowful for red-skin grievances, it's no sign he shouldn't try to head off red-skin deviltries, for it can't be denied the Injins are doing such things, and that chiefs are going around, in the words of the good book, like a roaring lion, seeking whom they may eat up. I was satisfied a long while ago that Tecumseh was going to visit these regions, and for no good neither."

As he uttered the last words, he dropped lightly to the earth, to hurry away in the wood as swiftly and yet as noiselessly as a bird. Not a twig crackled—hardly a branch rustled as his shadowy form rapidly approached the camp-fire. He showed no signs of hesitation until within twenty yards, when, halting a moment, he ascended a tree. There, perched among the branches, he had an unobstructed view of the scene below, while his own form was secure from observation. The ceremonies we are about to describe took place in a large open square, but a short distance from the main village. Among the participants were recognized some of the most renowned chiefs of the Creek and Shawnee tribes.

The first form noticed was that of the great Tecumseh himself, who led the way, the warriors following, one in the footsteps of the other. "The Creeks, in dense masses, stood on one side of the path, but the Shawnees noticed no one; they marched to the pole in the center of the square, and then turned to the left. At each angle of the square, Tecumseh took from his pouch some tobacco and sumach, and dropped it on the ground; his warriors performed the same ceremony. This they repeated three times as they marched around the square. Then they approached the flag-pole in the center, circled around it three times, and, facing the north, threw tobacco and sumach on a small fire, burning as usual near the base of the pole. Upon this they emptied their pouches. They then marched in the same order to the council, or king's house, (as it was termed in ancient times,) and drew up before it. The Big Warrior and leading men were sitting there. The Shawnee chieftain sounded his war-whoop—a most diabolical yell—and each of his followers responded. Tecumseh then presented to the Big

Warrior a wampum-belt of five different-colored strands, which the Creek chief handed to his warriors, and it passed down the line. The Shawnee's pipe was then produced; it was large, long, and profusely decorated with shells, beads, and painted eagle and porcupine quills. It was lighted from the fire in the center, and slowly passed from the Big Warrior along the line.

"All this time not a word had been uttered—every thing was still as death: even the winds slept, and there was nothing heard but the gentle falling of the leaves. At length Tecumseh spoke, at first slowly and in sonorous tones, but he soon grew impassioned, and the words fell in avalanches from his lips, his eyes burned with supernatural luster, and his whole frame trembled with emotion. His voice resounded over the multitude—now sinking in low, musical whispers, now rising to its highest key, hurling out his words like a succession of thunderbolts. His countenance varied with his speech: sometimes a murderous smile, and for a brief interval a sentiment of profound sorrow pervaded it, and at the close a look of concentrated vengeance, such as might be supposed to distinguish the arch enemy of mankind.

"'In defiance of the white warriors of Ohio and Kentucky, I have traveled through their settlements, once our favorite hunting-grounds. No war-whoop was sounded, but there was blood on our knives. The pale-faces felt the blow, but knew not whence it came.

"'Accursed be the race that has seized on our country and made women of our warriors. Our fathers, from their tombs, reproach us as slaves and cowards. I hear them now in the wailing winds.

"'The Muscogee was once a mighty people. The Georgians trembled at our war-woop, and the maidens of my tribe, in the distant lakes, sung the prowess of your warriors and sighed for their embraces.

"'Now, your very blood is white; your tomahawks have no edge; your bows and arrows were buried with your fathers. Oh Muscogees, brethren of my mother! brush from your eyelids the sleep of slavery; once more strike for vengeance—once more for your country. The spirits of the mighty dead complain. The tears drop from the weeping skies. Let the white race perish.

"'They seize your land; they corrupt your women; they trample on the ashes of your dead!

"'Back whence they came, upon a trail of blood, they must be driven!

"'Back, back—ay, into the great water whose accursed waves brought them to our shores!

"'Burn their dwellings! Destroy their stock! Slay their

wives and children! The red-man owns the country, and the pale-face must never enjoy it.

"'War now! War forever! War upon the living! War upon the dead! Dig their corpses from the grave! Our country must give no rest to the white man's bones.

"'All the tribes of the North are dancing the war-dance; Two mighty warriors across the seas will send us arms.

"'Tecumseh will soon return to his country. My prophets shall tarry with you. They will stand between you and the bullets of your enemies. When the white man approaches you, the yawning earth shall swallow him up.

"'Soon shall you see my arm of fire stretched athwart the sky. I will stamp my foot at Tippecanoe, and the very earth shall shake!'

"The effect of this irresistible burst of eloquence upon the wild, superstitious and warlike 'Stoics of the woods' can scarcely be conceived. They shook and swayed like the tempest-tossed ocean, and a thousand tomahawks were brandished in the air. Even the Big Warrior, who for years had been faithful to the whites, grasped his knife with a spasmodic clutch of his huge hand, and his breast heaved with the mighty passion which was convulsing him. It was only by an almost superhuman struggle that he mastered his feelings, and presented at the close of the speech the only unmoved countenance in that immense multitude.

"Although Tecumseh's mother was a Creek, and he understood the tongue, yet he spoke in the northern dialect, and his words were afterward interpreted by an Indian linguist; yet, had his listeners been deaf and dumb, the effect would have been none the less. His impassioned gestures, the lightning of his eye, the wonderful play of his countenance, were such as to need no interpreter—they were the language of his mighty soul and could not be mistaken."

But, to the great chieftain's voice, more than any thing else, was this whirlwind of emotion attributable. The most powerful-toned organ was scarce its equal in volume, compass and force. At times it was clear, ringing and musical as a chime of bells; and then again the whispering zephyr that stirred the leaves was not fainter. When a silence like that of death rested on his auditors, and his lips barely moved, his eyes suddenly glowed with a furious fire, and shot the most scathing lightning over their heads, and the words were hurled from his enormous chest like successive peals of thunder.* His power over

---

* This is scarce exaggeration. The voice of Tecumseh was not the least wonderful of the characteristics of that extraordinary being. When he spoke, the surrounding atmosphere was *full* of the sound, and the waves shuddered and trembled as if shaken by a score of organs.

the dusky orators, for the time being, was absolute. Every eye was drawn toward him as the loadstone draws the magnet, and the surging sea of passion in his own breast had its counterpart in theirs.

The ceremony took place in a large open square near the Creek village, where their warriors had assembled, and where there was abundant room for all to hear the words of the Shawnee chief. The numerous torches that lit up the scene like the light of the noonday sun, added greatly to the effect of the different ceremonies, and to an observer there was a semblance of terrible reality in all that transpired, which rendered it doubly impressive.

The result of Tecumseh's eloquence was, perhaps, as great upon the white man ensconced in that tree, as upon any of the Indian auditors. For a while he maintained his seat as stoically as if preparing for sleep; but as the Shawnee progressed, his frame caught the emotion that seemed borne upon the very air. He drew his breath hard between his set teeth, and trembled as though about to fall from his seat. As the last words of the orator rang out with startling fierceness, his feelings became uncontrollable, and he dropped to the ground and ran with the speed of the wind through the wood. It was not till he had gone several hundred yards that he halted.

"Oh! that was awful!" he exclaimed, drawing a deep breath. "If I had stayed there ten minutes longer, I would have landed right among 'em with a tearing yell. No wonder they are all afraid of Tecumseh! I would as lief stand before the muzzle of Spitfire at twenty yards distant, as to meet the fire that comes out of his eyes. Oh! I must get rid of this within me or I shall brust!"

Whipping out his knife, he plunged it again and again in the soft earth, accompanying it by such ejaculations. "Take that, you white man! How does that suit? You will learn better than to persecute the poor Injin."

An observer would have taken him for a lunatic, so whimsical and ludicrous were his antics. Not only did he cut and tear the ground, but, catching the shrubbery in his hands, he wrenched off the twigs, tore them up by the roots, and flung them about his head. He carried his apparent frenzy so far as to beat the earth with his head and fists. He turned summersets, rolled over and over, gnashed his teeth, threw handfuls of dirt and leaves hither and thither, until he paused, completely exhausted. It was thus he rid himself of the novel effects of Tecumseh's harangue.

## CHAPTER II.

### THE EVENTS OF A NIGHT.

> Let us meet,
> And question this most bloody piece of work.
> To know it further.         MACBETH.

AFTER thus freeing himself from the effects of the chieftain's eloquence, the adventurer arose to his feet, cool and unexcited. One of those half scornful smiles, which so frequently crossed his countenance, now illuminated it as he muttered:

"'Twas a foolish piece of business, but it couldn't be helped. No one could 've made me do it but Tecumseh, and I'll not deny but what he could do it ag in; but, I must away to Lindower's, as he is expecting me."

It was still early in the night—lacking several hours of the turn. The ragged clouds which had been driving across the heavens in the commencement of the evening, had been gradually clearing away for some time, and the light of the moon was now strong and steady. The luminary was riding high in the sky, as if seeking to rise above the tumultuous masses that had so obscured her face; and, although by no means in the full, the air with its metal-like clearness conducted its rays to the earth, seemingly without dissipating a single pencil of light. The river was revealed so distinctly as to reflect the smallest object upon its surface, while the obscurity of the wood seemed absolutely impenetrable from the contrast.

A few minutes after the soliloquy just given, a dark object drifted from the shadows of the northern shore, out into the moonlit stream. A careful scrutiny would have satisfied an eye not too suspicious, that it was some log, borne downward by the sluggish current. Nothing resembling a human form could be distinguished, although the object itself seemed about the length of a common Indian canoe. It drifted slowly, and seemingly without the least guidance; but for all this, there was something in the very course of the object that was calculated to excite suspicion. Instead of floating in a direct line with the stream, it was gradually sheering off from the shore where it was first seen, and making its way across the river. There was no breeze to account for this freak, but now and then a sparkling of the water beside the object, as if made by a fish coming to the surface, was enough to show there was human agency at work.

The object drifted downward for a half-hour, by which time

it had approached the dark line of shade upon the southern shore. Into this it slowly floated, until entirely enveloped by the obscurity, when the form of a man rose to the sitting position, and touching the water with a long Indian paddle, the canoe shot in to the shore like the sudden turn of the sparrow. The feet of the occupant touched the bank at the same instant that the prow did, and seizing the latter in one hand, the canoe slid its entire length upon dry ground, as if borne onward only by the impulse of the paddle. The latter was placed carefully in it, and both covered by the dense shrubbery.

"There is no log handy," soliloquized the owner, "and this will have to answer. Even as it is, it will take a keener eye than a Creek's to lay his hand upon it, although I incline to believe them shining orbs of Tecumseh would point out the place while he stood on t'other side."

The next instant the speaker was making his way through the forest, with the same noiseless strides that had characterized his approach to the Indian council. At intervals, his lips slightly parted, and he communed with himself; but his words were no louder than the whispering zephyrs overhead, and could have been heard only by the one who uttered them. When it lacked about an hour of midnight, he reached the margin of a clearing, several acres in extent, where he halted and commenced reconnoitering. In the center of this open space stood a settler's cabin, two stories in hight, and pierced by several small windows. It was constructed entirely of logs, including the roof, the latter being rapidly shelving, and projecting a foot beyond the sides of the house. The door, composed of heavy puncheon slabs, was as massive and ponderous as if sawed from the side of the structure itself, while the small windows, scarcely larger than a single pane of glass, resembled the iron-barred casements of some old embattled castle. The clearing, which surrounded the cabin for many yards upon all sides, bore signs of the hand of the husbandman in every part. A small patch of corn had been so thriftily nurtured that the stalks were already several inches above the surface, and in other spots the rich virgin soil was distilling its subtle strength into the numerous vegetables which generally are found in the garden of the toiling settler. This scene of honest frugality was inclosed by a strong fence of brush, strengthened by piles of stones gathered from the small clearing and wood. Numerous stumps, also, that had been wrested from the earth, with their ragged, prong-like roots attached, were flung upon this protecting wall, so that the hunter had in fact inclosed himself by a parapet impregnable to the mischievous animals which so annoy the farmer in a new country. Several charred stumps, too firmly imbedded to be extracted by the single strength of the settler, still disfigured the clearing, and stood out from the rapidly-sprouting vegetation, like black sentinels keeping guard over that oasis in the vast wilderness.

On such a scene as this did the man gaze. He paused, as if in doubt, gazed eagerly and closely around at every spot. There was a chilling, portentous gloom in the dreadful silence that had settled upon the cabin and clearing—the very air, unstirred by a single breath, was laden with suspicion. He stood a moment, his eyes riveted upon the structure, as though he would pierce its very walls and view the interior, and then, as was his wont, he commenced muttering to himself:

"'Tis extronnery—certainly extronnery that my stummick should feel so heavy that I must heave a long breath when I look upon Lindower's cabin there—it's extronnery, sartin. It can't be the Creeks have been at their devilments, when Tecumseh husn't spoke an hour ago. It's now about the turn of night, and it stands to reason that Lindower and Laura have gone to sleep long ago; but I can't shake off the idee that something's wrong. When they come to these parts two years ago, I told them I should be here about this time, and they should have l'arnt to expect me, for I'm ginerally as true to my promises as Spitfire is to her ahn. P'raps, though, they've forgotten, and I'll try the call Lindower and me used when on a hunt in the Shawnee country."

As he spoke, the man held his hand, in the form of a tunnel, to his mouth, and gave forth the wavering, dismal hoot of the owl, repeating it three times, and abruptly ending the fourth call as though the bird had been suddenly frightened during its utterance. Then clasping both hands on the upper part of the gun-barrel, he leaned his weight forward upon it, and listened and watched. For fully ten minutes he was not less motionless than the tree-trunk beside him. Satisfied then that his signal had accomplished nothing, he repeated it in precisely the same manner as before, and then watched and listened as intently for some sign from the cabin that it had been recognized. The last thrilling notes were still lingering on the air, when a human face, or the shadow of one, slowly swept past the upper window, and vanished as suddenly as it had made its appearance. It was not the face of a white man or woman, but of an Indian, as if convulsed by mortal agony, and the black eyes gleamed and glowed with a deadly fire, as they swept past and disappeared in the darkness like two twin stars swallowed up by the folds of a cloud.

The window at which this apparition appeared was thrown into shadow by its position; and, although the gaze of the man was fixed directly upon it as the one from which he expected a reply to his signal, the gloom was so great that it entirely scaped him. Had it been his expected friend, the waving of a handkerchief would have assured him that all was right; but he waited until he felt it was vain to expect such a recognition.

"It looks bad—it looks bad," he muttered, shaking his head. "Gorman Lindower would have known the meaning of that hoot, if he was in his cabin, and his sister Laura sleeps so light that the first call would have awakened her. I much fear there is mischief afoot."

He now circled round the cabin, viewing it from every attainable position, and even went so far as to ascend a tree, far above the roof, from which he gazed down upon it. The logs were as they had appeared when he saw them six months before, and now that he had a full view of the clearing, he descried no disturbance or unusual appearance in it; but his eye was attracted by a break in the fence, on the opposite side from him, which, in his scrutiny of the cabin itself, had hitherto escaped his notice. Before descending to examine this more closely, he broke a large rotten limb, and swung it outward so as to fall upon the roof, striking with a dull crash, breaking in numerous pieces, and sliding to the ground. He then listened to ascertain whether any one was moving within, but he heard no sound, although, had he been in a favorable position, he would have seen the same frightful and distorted face appear and vanish at the window, with an expression as if appealing against molestation while undergoing some physical agony.

"They're gone—that's settled," said the man, cautiously descending; and the house is empty; and so, without stopping to look at the break in the fence, I'll take a look inside."

Still, it was against his nature to approach the cabin without more circumlocution, and he viewed the windows and door again and again, and hurled a stone against the latter. Approaching the rupture in the fence, although he had intended to omit this step, he examined it critically and minutely. To his experienced eye, it was evident the passage had been made ly tearing the brush apart, and flinging the stumps and stones aside. That it had been hastily done was apparent from the manner in which the latter were scattered around, and that it had been done by hostile hands, was certain from the numerous moccasin tracks in the soft earth in the clearing. It required but a few minutes to satisfy him that a band of Indians had clambered or leaped into the inclosure, and, after completing their work of plunder, and probably death, had cleared the way through the fence for an unobstructed passage into the forest again.

"The varmints have been at work," he muttered. "Poor Lindower and Laura have found the trouble they was told to expect when they come so far out into a new country 'specially when there was signs of a gineral trouble among them."

A slight pressure forced the door open, and he noiselessly entered. The moon was upon his back, and its light entering behind him, lit up the room in every part. A single glance showed him the plunderers had been at work. A feather-bed had been ripped open and its contents scattered over the floor, while broken crockery, chairs and different articles of furniture were strewn around. A careful search, however, failed to reveal any signs of blood upon the floor or sides of the cabin, and he concluded that his two friends had been simply carried off as prisoners.

"Yaa, the skunks have carried them off, and, judging from signs in these parts, should say they can be accused of injuring the man's furniture in the bargain. How is it they haven't burnt up his cabin to make a complete thing of it, is more than I can tell at present. P'raps they're consid'ring the proposition to occupy it themselves." Here the man paused to indulge in a laugh at his own humor, and then resumed more seriously: "I'm afraid it's a bad job for Lindower and the gal; but I'll take a look above and then strike out in the woods, for the General needs my sarvices."

With this he stepped to one corner of the room and commenced ascending to the upper story, by means of a piece of mechanism half-stairs and half-ladder. In doing this, he held his inseparable rifle in his left hand, and grasped the cross-pieces above him, one after the other, with his right, so as to facilitate his upward progress. He had taken but a step or two, when his hand came in contact with something, which sent a cold chill through his entire body. He dropped back again to the floor, and examined the loathsome substance. As he expected, found it was blood. He rubbed it off with a quick, nervous movement, as though it were poison.

"That looks bad again," he mused. "It shows there's been desprit work, and hard fighting going on. It may have been Laura's, as she was trying to get away from the villains; but I'll wager Spitfire here against a revolutioner musket that Gorman Lindower made the head of one of them pay for it, allowing that they served her so."

He now recommenced the ascent, carefully avoiding any contact with the clotted blood. The upper story was divided into two apartments, and as his head appeared above the opening in the floor, he cast a rapid glance around the first room. The situation of this was such that the moon failed to light up every portion, and he was compelled to a minute examination before he was satisfied of its condition. Nothing was disturbed, and the bed, standing upon a rough frame-work, was as crumpled as though the tidy hands of its maker were the last object that had touched it.

"The ideas of a Creek's mind are as crooked as some of their paths. It's plain the villains wa'n't after plunder, for the most valyble part of Gorman's fixings are in this same story, and they haven't laid han is on any thing here. Ah's me! I wonder if *her* room is the same."

He now made his way into the apartment which, probably, had been occupied by Laura Lindower. This was pierced by a single window, and was lit somewhat better by the moonlight, although the eye could not take in every corner at a glance. As he looked toward the bed, he startled as he saw it was disturbed as though lain upon by some person. He recoiled a step, fearing it might be dangerous to approach, and endeavored to penetrate every part of the room with his gaze. When his eyes became accustomed to the semi-darkness, he discovered that each corner was empty. The room was a simple rectangle, occupying one-half of the upper portion of the house, and was without any closet or cupboard that could offer concealment for a person, so that he was satisfied, if any one was in the room, he must be under the bed. As he stood in the doorway, he stooped and looked under this; but his eyes were not strong enough to pierce the obscurity, and he could assure himself only by actual examination. This was rather a hazardous attempt; for, should any enemy be there, his movements could not be seen, while his own would be visible in the moonlit room.

But, as it was the only means by which he could free himself of that uncomfortable sensation of not knowing to a certainty that he was alone in the appartment, he determined to make the examination. He was as confident that this portion of the room was empty, but was not rid of the uneasy fact that he might be mistaken. Seizing the stock of his rifle firmly in both hands, he pushed its muzzle as far under the bed as he could reach without approaching too close, and attempted to make a wide sweep from the head to the foot. The barrel had not passed one-half of the distance, when it encountered a sudden obstruction, and in an instant was violently wrenched from his hand. For a second or two the angular arms of the surprised man beat the air with the quickness of lightning, and he slid backward several feet as if impelled by the power of his antagonist. But it was a voluntary movement, and he had regained possession of his rifle. Quickly cocking it, he dropped upon one knee, and pointing it under the bed, said in a low, decided voice:

"White or red, speak! or I'll let moonlight through you!"

There was no answering word or movement, and the deep

rapid breathing only betrayed the presence of another being in this room.

"Once more I command you to speak, or as sure as Spitfire is pointed at you, I fire!"

An ominous silence still reigned in the room, and the speaker's finger already was pressing upon the trigger, with the full determination to execute his threat, when the Indian rolled from under the bed, and looking toward his disturber, said, as he lay upon his back:

"Injin hurt—Nockwynoe much hurt!"

"That's plain to be seen," said the white man, lowering the stock, but still keeping the muzzle pointed toward the savage. "That's plain to be seen; and, though your dress and paint show you to be a bloody-minded Creek upon the war-path, and your being under Miss Laura's bed doesn't preach very well for you, still, I'm not the one to refuse what comfort I can give you. Shall I fix up that ugly-looking cut?"

"Creek hurt very much—white brother stop blood."

"That I couldn't refuse my meanest enemy, and I'll do what I can."

"White brother come nearer—fix hurt," said the savage, eagerly.

"Now, just see here," said the white man, with considerable asperity in his tone, "just take that blasted looking knife out of your hand, or I don't come any nearer."

"Creek no hurt white brother," said the savage, speaking rapidly, and fixing his eye upon him.

"Then the knife can do you no good. I've seen too much of Creek treachery to fuss around you with that weapon in your hand; so, I'll be clever enough to relieve you from it."

The white man reached forward, and taking the knife by the point, gently drew the haft through the hand which closed unequally upon it, as if the owner were still in doubt whether he should allow it to pass from his possession. When the former held it in his fingers, he tossed it lightly over his head, it falling upon its point, and remaining sticking upright in the floor. Satisfying himself that the Creek had nothing else in his possession which he could treacherously use, he approached and examined the wound.

"It's a bad cut, but I don't see that it should be the death of you. From the style in which the thing is finished up, I should say it was done by the knife of Gorman Lindower. I mind me now, he had a curious twist to his knife when he used it, and I see the marks here. Was it not so, Creek?"

"White man's knife long—strike hard!" replied the Indian, fixing his glittering orbs upon him.

"Just so - Gorman has a strong arm, and I don't need to be

told of it; but while talking, Creek, or Nockwynee, as you call yourself, I'll tend to that cut of yourn."

Without further ceremony, the white man proceeded to tear one of the linen sheets in threads, and bandage the wound of the Indian. In doing this, he saw there was already blood upon the bed, as though the savage had sought to rest himself upon it, until he heard the approaching footsteps, when he had concealed himself. In a few moments he had stanched the flow, and saw that the wounded man felt easier, his jealous eyes constantly following his every movement, as he busied himself beside him. Finally he asked, in hurried tones:

"What name?"

"Wal, Nockwynee, it's a long time since I've used the Christian name that was the first one that was given me; and, seeing that it would do no good for you to know it, I'll mention the one by which I've been known along the frontier for the past ten years. I'm called *The Forest Spy*."

There was a perceptible start in the Indian's manner, and his keen gaze became more penetrating, if possible, than before, as he said:

"Forest Spy great hunter—Nockwynee know him—he stay with Nockwynee to-night."

This request of the savage for the white man to remain by him until morning, might have been nothing more than the simple wish of a wounded man for company, during the desolate hours; but the Forest Spy viewed it in a far different light. It awakened the strongest suspicion in his mind that the Creek was bringing his habitual treachery into play. Well aware of this trait, so characteristic of this tribe in particular, the action of the savage in wishing to retain his knife, while he was performing the offices of the good Samaritan over him, convinced him that he would not hesitate to take his life, if opportunity offered; and, since the Forest Spy had revealed his identity, the request of the Creek placed him on his guard.

This disposition of the savage, when receiving the kindest offers of the white man, would have summarily ended the good-will of almost any one; but it was different with the man in question. Stooping over the Creek, he carefully lifted him in his arms, and placed him on the bed, turning a cover over him. The savage flung the latter off again, and said:

"No want cover—Nockwynee no white man."

"A1 very well. Now, Nockwynee, how was it you got hurt?"

"White man's knife long—knife sharp."

"Did they kill the white man and the girl?"

"No kill—carry 'em off. Two, t'ree, so many Creek take 'em away," said the savage, holding up the fingers and thumbs of both hands.

"I s'picioned as much. What made them carry 'em off?"

"White man no right here," replied the savage, with great energy. "Creek hunting-ground. Tecumseh drive all white men off—back in the sea."

"The Shawnee's deviltry has begun to work," mused the Spy. "He's been stirring the villains up. But what will they do with the white man and girl?"

"Keep 'em till all whites killed—maybe burn 'em—push 'em in sea."

"Where have they taken them?"

"Nockwynee know nottin'; leave him here," replied the Indian, quickly.

"Why leave Nockwynee here? Are they coming back after him?"

"No come back;—leave Nockwynee here till he get well."

The Forest Spy shook his head doubtingly, and half smiled, but made no reply. He glanced at the Indian's hunting-knife, still sticking on its point in the corner, and muttered:

"'Tis an omen that the house is to be visited again by some one. The villains, after getting the plunder and the boy and gal at a safe distance, will come back and take the savage off with them—most likely not afore daylight. They've put him up here to rest easy, and he's trying to keep me here until they return, when he cac'lates there'll be one less white man to push into the sea. Ah's me! it's a cur'ous red-skin whose heart isn't reached by kindness. I'll nuss him further, and see if he don't thaw out."

The speaker took the other pillow that lay like a snow-drift at the head of the bed, and doubling it, placed it under the head of the Creek, making his position much more comfortable and easy.

"Can I do any thing more for Nockwynee?" he asked, in a kindly tone.

"Nottin' more," replied the Creek, who now lay breathing regularly, and who kept up a fixed gaze upon his white friend. The eyes of the latter did not once encounter his, but he knew, nevertheless, the jealous scrutiny that was kept up. In a few minutes the Creek appeared to rest uneasily, turning his head and moving his body.

"Shall I fix the bed for you?"

"No; nottin' more," he replied, exhibiting great nervousness in his reply.

The Forest Spy well knew what the trouble was. The good feelings of his Indian nature were beginning to assert themselves, and he was not surprised at the question:

"White brother stay with Nockwynee?"

"Does Nockwynee wish him to?"

The Indian did not reply for a moment. Then suddenly rising to the sitting posture, he said, with great earnestness:

"White man go—Creek coming—kill him when find he is here."

"Ha! ha!" laughed the undisturbed Spy, "I knew the Inj'n would soon show itself. I'll take your advice, Nockwynee, and leave soon."

"Go now—go—Creek coming," repeated the Indian, with greater energy than before. "Creek—two—t'ree—so many (again holding up both hands) coming—soon be here!"

The startling energy of the savage warned the Forest Spy that he had been mistaken in supposing his companions would not return until morning, and that every moment he delayed, he was rendering his situation the more perilous. Even now his enemies might be in the clearing; this possibility took a fearful probability in his mind, when the Indian, maintaining the sitting posture, and in the same energetic manner, said:

"Look out—Creek may be near."

The white man had determined to "look out" of the windows and either end of the house before thus warned to, and he now proceeded to do so. Walking to the small opening which served to admit the light in the apartment in which he then stood, he made a careful survey of such a part of the clearing and wood as came under his vision. The moon was so bright that every blade of corn, every stone, was visible, up to the brush-fence, where the shadows of the wood wrapped every thing in one dark, impenetrable field of obscurity. His eyes wandered along the margin of the wood several times, but he failed to detect any thing to excite his alarm; and he determined, if the view from the opposite end of the house revealed nothing more, to make the attempt to reach the forest. As he turned to pass to the other apartment, the wounded Creek asked, with much interest:

"See nottin'?—no Creek yet?"

"Not on that side of the house, Nockwynee; but I don't know what this window will show."

The view from this window took in that portion of the fence which had been torn down by the savages; and he had scarcely glanced at it when the Creek asked:

"See no Creek? Nottin' there?"

"If there isn't a half-dozen Creeks skulking along the wood yonder, then I'll smash Spitfire!" said the Forest Spy, turning his head as he spoke, but maintaining his position at the window.

"What do? what white man do?" asked the savage, endeavoring to rise and get on his feet.

"Tut, tut, man," said the other, raising his hand deprecatingly. "Just keep your place on your bed, for they're your own brothers, and don't expect you would do any thing, especially as you're not able. Just lay still there, and I'll make the effort to crawl out of this hole, for I've been in tighter places afore. The villains have s'picioned something, and p'raps have seen my tracks in the earth, as I didn't take particular pains to hide 'em. Nockwynce, I have plenty ammunition; suppose I consider myself besieged, and make this a fort, and keep off the dogs as long as I can?"

This question was only an artifice of the Spy, to probe more satisfactorily the feelings and disposition of his Indian companion. He had no serious intention of carrying out the course he had hinted, for he well knew it was absolutely impossible. Should Nockwynce evince a willingness to assist him, he had no rifle; and the utmost vigilance could not prevent his enemies from surrounding and burning the cabin over their heads. As yet the savages only suspected something out of the usual course of things within the house, and the Forest Spy by no means despaired of outwitting them in the end. The reply of the Indian was as he expected:

"No shoot—Creek kill—two, t'ree—so many (holding up his hands)—burn cabin—take scalp—no shoot."

"Your counsel is good, Nockwynee, and shall be followed."

The savage, apparently satisfied, dropped back upon the bed, and listened. While the white man was holding this fragmentary conversation with him, he had never once left his post at the window, turning his head only as he spoke. The cause of his decisive reply to the first question, was no less than an Indian, who was seen to move in a bent position from one of the loose stumps to another. While speaking he had counted five different forms, constantly and stealthily changing their position and gradually approaching the cabin. He could have easily shot one, but such, as stated above, was not his intention. The window in the opposite room, in which the Indian lay, was the one thrown into shadow, and the Forest Spy felt that if his escape was effected, it must be by means of that.

Occasionally he stepped hastily to it and peered out, and was gratified to find no signs of his enemies upon that side. From this he judged the Creeks knew of the room in which their wounded companion lay, and were, consequently, approaching from the opposite direction. This was the wisest course: for in doing so, the only opening through which a rifle could be directed toward them was the window referred to, which, under the full light of the moon, would instantly betray such as attempt; while, if the *sides* of the cabin were taken instead of the *ends*, the Creeks would expose their bodies to a dozen port holes, through which, for aught they knew, so many messengers of death might be hurled upon them at any moment. The Forest Spy now approached the shaded window and carefully removed the sash. There were but two panes in it, and its size was barely sufficient to admit the passage of his body. He effected this without noise, and a minute after, heard the soft, cat-like tread of a moccasin on the floor of the lower room.

## CHAPTER III.

### A NIGHT OF PERIL AND OF ACTION.

Dark night, that from the eye his function takes,
The eye more quick of apprehension makes.
MIDSUMMER NIGHT'S DREAM.

WHEN the suppressed step of the Indian was heard on the lower floor, the Forest Spy leaned as far out of the window as possible, and holding his rifle for an instant by the muzzle, dropped it to the ground. As the weapon left his hand, the lower portion was but a few feet from the earth, and it descended this short distance without losing its uprightness, falling upon the stock, and tipping lightly against the house as if placed there by the owner himself. This done, the latter drew his head back and waited to see whether it attracted attention. It appeared to have been unheard, for he saw no one appear; but, in the few seconds necessarily consumed in doing this, the footsteps in the lower room had increased by the sounds to full a dozen, and were now heard pattering upon the floor, like the passing hither and thither of so many cats.

There was not a moment to be lost, for the next instant the heads of the Creeks might appear. Running his feet quickly and noiselessly through the opening, he forced himself out until he hung by his hands, when, balancing himself in this position for a few moments, he dropped lightly to the ground, and, seizing his rifle, ran a few yards, and dropped flat on his face behind a large stump. As he did so, he heard a slight disturbance at the window he had left; and, although he could detect nothing suspicious, yet from the peculiar suppressed rattle, he rightly judged it was made by Nockwynee in replacing the sash, so as to conceal all evidence of his departure.

Most fortunately his escape from the building had not attracted the attention of the Creeks; but he saw, with some misgivings, he forms of three Indians issue from the door, and take their position at the corner of the house, as if detailed to act as sentinels. Their position was such that they were not twenty feet distant, and he was only hid from their view by the intervening stump. He could not change his situation a foot unless under their very eye; and as he saw in the hands of each a gleaming rifle-barrel, he had no disposition to make that attempt at present. In a few moments, one of the Creeks disappeared around the corner of the house, and the remaining two commenced a sort of conversation. The Forest Spy understood the Creek dialect, although he had chosen to conceal the fact from Nockwynee, and now and then caught a word or two of the speakers. He heard the names of the "pale-faces," "white men," and more often that of the great Shawnee chief Tecumseh. In a few minutes, however, they ceased conversing, apparently at the suggestion of some one inside the cabin.

The prolonged stay of the Creeks within the house satisfied the Forest Spy that every moment he remained he was imperiling his safety, and that it would never do for him to wait until the savages came out again. A search could not fail to reveal the marks of his feet, and his precarious hiding-place. He determined to make the attempt to escape at once. Feeling cautiously around, his hand rested upon a small pebble, which, with a sort of jerking motion, he hurled over the cabin. He plainly heard the rattling sound it produced by striking a blade of corn, and it also attracted the attention of the two sentinels, who turned their heads and walked slowly in that direction. As quick as thought, the man arose on his hands and knees, and, imitating the motion of the baboon, half jumped and half leaped a few yards, sheering around another stump, and dropping as flatly behind it, as if he had been flung there by the hand of a giant.

The Forest Spy was now about one-half the distance between the cabin and the wood. His movements had been unobserved by his enemies. Fearing momentarily that these would issue forth, and render his case hopeless, he determined to resort to the same stratagem that had just helped him so well. Feeling around he secured a stone somewhat larger than the other, and using all the strength he dare summon at such a time, again "jerked" it toward the cabin. Instead of passing over, however, the distance was so great that it struck against the eaves, and fell directly at the feet of one of the sentinels. With a guttural exclamation he picked it up, and, in company with his companion, started toward the very stump from which it had come.

The instant their intention was seen, the man sprang to his

feet and started on a rapid run for the opening in the fence, the Creeks setting up a shout and trying to intercept him. Several others came from the cabin and joined in the pursuit. Knowing by the silence of their guns that their object was to capture him, the white man bent all his energies toward reaching the friendly opening ahead. He was very fleet of foot, and had the advantage by several rods, so that he was counting rather confidently upon his escape, when he discerned the hated forms of two Creeks, as they sprung from the obscurity of the wood, and entered the clearing by means of the very gateway toward which he was so laboriously directing his flight.

This was so unexpected, that, for a moment, the fugitive was taken aback; but, he did not cease running for a second, although literally hemmed in by his enemies. He had slackened his speed when the two savages appeared in front, and now swerved to the left, and commenced a race something similar to what a horse might be supposed to make when set upon by a score of wolves, and inclosed in a field of several acres. He doubled and feinted with such quickness and skill, that the savages saw the only way to secure him was by closing upon him from all sides. Against this the Forest Spy called into play every energy of his body and all the sagacity of his mind.

He noticed the two Creeks maintained their position in the opening, so as to prevent his eluding them by means of that, and the others, in spite of his exertions, were slowly but surely environing him. He ran his eye quickly around, and, detecting a spot in the fence somewhat depressed below its usual line, he determined to make the attempt to leap it; but, to his unspeakable chagrin, at the very second he formed this resolution, two other Indians took their position directly before it, as if the intention had flashed across their minds at the same time.

But he had the choice of ceasing his efforts and voluntarily surrendering, or of making the passage through the fence in the face of the opposition. Setting up a yell of defiance, he brandished his clubbed rifle, and again doubling, made directly toward the rent in the fence, as if he had resolved to press through the guard. The whole body of pursuers now strained themselves to cut him off, and several succeeded in getting themselves in front of him. He kept on, however, with untiring speed, until a collision between himself and those in the front seemed unavoidable, when, with the quickness of lightning, he again doubled on his course, and shot off with the speed of the antelope, at right angles to the direction he had thus far kept. A sort of half-howl and yell, given as much in admiration of his skill as of the rage they felt at their repeated fal ures to lay hands upon him, followed this movement; while the Creeks changed their course and poured tumultuously after him, his stratagem, however, giving him the lead of all, by several yards.

The two Indians had not left the favorable spot in the fence during the excitement of the chase; but now, when they saw the fugitive bursting toward them with tremendous velocity, they were thrilled by the sight, and, almost unconsciously to themselves, advanced to meet him. When within a dozen feet of the nearest foe, the body of the flying man rose in the air, and went clear over his head, striking the ground within a few feet of the fence. He appeared to *ricochet* like a cannon ball, bounding completely over the obstruction and vanishing in the gloom of the forest.

The pursuing Creeks paused in blank astonishment at this wonderful feat, and with numerous expressions of admiration and rage returned to the cabin. They well knew it would be the hight of folly to pursue, in the trackless forest, one who had exhibited such consummate prowess and cunning when cooped up and surrounded in the clearing by them, and therefore refrained from the attempt.

Alighting safely upon the ground, the Forest Spy dropped into a leisurely walk, taking a direction toward the point on the river-bank where he had left his canoe, muttering as usual to himself.

"I'm right down rejoiced to discover there's some muscle on these bones, even if their owner is getting summat along in years. No doubt them Creek villains thought I needed to practice a while afore I could make that leap; but I've done better things than that. I made a bigger jump among the bluffs of the 'Hio in '93, when hard pressed by the Shawnees:—but, ah's me! I mush't brag."

His long, rapid strides were as noiseless as ever, his footsteps, from years of practice, being as firm and stealthy as those of the panther. They seemed to have acquired that singular faculty of doing what was required of them, without any oversight of the mind, after the first exercise of the volition. Now that his legs had commenced walking, the will slumbered until it was necessary to telegraph to them to cease their locomotion—this and similar ones being about the only messages ever sent, as these useful members needed no admonitions to exercise the utmost care in their movements.

"Ah's me! but this is bad business for the boy and gal," mused the hunter. "Gorman should have heeded the words of older heads than his; but I've much faith in the cunning of his arm. But Laura! how will it be with her?—heaven help me!"

He stopped suddenly in his walk, as a most startling thought flashed athwart his mind. He trembled for a moment, and remained standing, while his brow compressed and his face assumed a look of confused and perplexed pain. It cleared away in a minute, leaving the same calm, undisturbed expression, and he spoke as he moved forward somewhat slower than before:

"It's so! It struck me that several of them villains looked like cur'ous Creeks. Thar dress and two or three glimpses I had of thar war-paint wasn't Creek. No, s-i-r! they was Shawnees! The bloody-minded villains have commenced their deviltry. The Creeks would have never disturbed Gorman if they hadn't been set on and helped by them Shawnees that Tecumseh has brought down in these parts. This being the case," he resumed, after a few minutes' thought, "Laura will be taken north. Wal, perhaps it is as well, as I think the Gineral will need me up in that section, and p'raps I may do her a good turn, after all, while I'll answer that Gorman won't need any one to interfere for him."

Musing thus, and occasionally giving shape to his thoughts, the Forest Spy advanced rapidly along the river, and soon reached the spot where he had left his canoe. He stooped down, reached his hand under the bushes, fully expecting to lay it upon the object, when, to his unbounded astonishment, he found it was missing! Some one had removed it!

"That's mean and entirely onaccountable," he vexatiously exclaimed. "No Creek has done that either; some sneaking Shawnee has followed me over and run off with it. That comes from forgetting to be as careful as I ginerally am. Howsumever, I must take a look to see if that canoe is anywhere near at hand."

This conclusion was rather thought than expressed. He commenced making his way down-stream, through the tangled overhanging bushes and limbs. He knew if the canoe was on that side of the river it must be below him, as he could not have passed it in coming from the cabin. He had gone but a few rods when he distinguished the boat lying out in the stream, just on the boundary line of the shadow of the shore and the moonlit surface of the river. The current, thus close to the shore, was very sluggish, and the canoe was slowly floating with it, as though set loose by some one and abandoned. It was drifting sideways, and one half of it, from the bow to the center, was exposed to the light of the moon, which revealed to the penetrating eye of the Forest Spy his red Indian paddle only, resting in the bottom. He was sagacious enough to understand, however, that the slight uprising of the bow, and the depression of the stern, was caused by the weight of a man in the latter portion.

It was a little beyond midnight. There was not the slightest breath of air stirring, the surface of the river being as smooth and glistening as the polished mirror. The canoe, instead of working its way outward, floated a few inches inward, toward shore. The Forest Spy lost even the imperfect view he had of the interior; and, satisfied that it would neither come any nearer, nor drift out further, he twice raised "Spitfire" and pointed it at the gloom in the stern, with the intention of firing, and ridding the canoe of its occupant. But some power restrained his arm, and he determined to do no such deed until assured to a certainty that it *was* an enemy that had taken possession of his property.

With this resolution, he removed his hunting-cap, and, sustaining himself by means of his left hand, he reached as far out as convenient with the right, and commenced swaying the cap slowly backward and forward. This movement set a current of air in motion, which, slight as it was, soon had a visible effect upon the canoe. The beautiful structure was poised so nicely and delicately upon the surface of the water, that the slightest breath of air was sufficient to set it in motion, the same as the exertions of a small boat would move a steamship, in calm water, with its ponderous machinery and mighty freight; and the invisible touch of the atmosphere upon its side, scarcely enough to have fanned the light of a candle, began moving it outward, slowly at first, but so surely, that the hunter replaced his cap, satisfied that the slight propulsion would accomplish all he could desire.

Three-fourths of the canoe had emerged into view, when its occupant suddenly rose to the sitting position and looked around him, betraying in the movement the head and shoulders of an Indian in war-paint. The rifle of the Forest Spy was instantly at his shoulder, but as suddenly lowered, as he recognized the savage, and he called in a subdued voice:

"Come in, come in, Musconondon; it's myself."

The savage immediately lifted the paddle, and by a dexterous movement ran it in to shore, where its real owner stepped in and said:

"Give me the paddle, Musconondon, and I'll send the boat to a spot where we can talk. I s'pose you're from the Gineral."

The savage nodded his head by way of reply, and, under the skillful guidance of the white man, the boat shot in under a mass of shrubbery lying upon the surface of the water, and which rattled and closed about them as densely and compactly as the cotton does around the bullet that enters it. Feeling that they were now safe, Forest Spy said:

"Now, Musconondon, I'll bear your message."

"No message—chip speak," said the savage, taking a small, thin piece of shingle from his mouth and handing it to his companion.

It was so dark that the latter recognized it only by the sense of touch; but, as he had received messages from the same man in such a form on more than one previous occasion, he understood perfectly what it meant.

"So the General trusts a shingle sooner than Musconondon," he chuckled. "I s'pose, howsomever, it's the best plan, as it seems harder for you to get the hang of our English gibberish than for Nockwynce. As there isn't much light here, and the matter can be put off till the sun comes, we'll lay down and wait till morning."

"No wait—Musconondon must go. Suu must no find in Creek country."

"Wal, wal, as you say, then; I'll drop you on t'other side, though I would fain wait until the morn had got summat further toward the earth. There's Shawnees and Creeks moving on both sides of the river; but you shall go—you shall go."

Without any more words, he backed the canoe from its concealment by a powerful sweep of the paddle, and shot off across the river.

"Lay down, Musconondon—lay down; there's no occasion for the villains to see both of us."

His Indian companion did as directed, and under the vigorous skill of Forest Spy, the canoe skimmed over the river, like the swallow that tips the surface as it flits past. He moved in a straight line until within fifty feet of the other shore, when he turned at right angles, and sent the canoe with incredible velocity for full a hundred yards directly down-stream, and at a uniform distance from the land. When he had accomplished this, he suddenly sheered it in to shore, and Musconondon, rising to his feet, sprung nimbly out, and vanished in the forest without speaking a word, while Forest Spy swept the boat around with the quickness of lightning, and in an instant was far out in the river.

This precaution was taken to avoid running into the hands of enemies whom he believed to be waiting upon the shore at the point where they supposed he would land. He saw, a moment later, that this very course had saved Musconondon as well as himself, for he soon heard a shout of defiance from the former, which showed, plainly enough, that a whole horde were in pursuit.

"Run, you villains," chuckled the hunter, ceasing his paddling for a moment. "I'll answer for his safety. The Shawnee or Creek isn't born that has the fleetness of Musconondon and in the windings of *that* wood, a she-painter would kill herself with rage at the tricks and capers he would serve her."

His words were accompanied by a dull plash in the water, and nearly at the same moment two canoes, containing four Indians each, emerged swiftly into view, one taking a direction down, and the other up stream, so as to surround him, (if the expression be allowable,) and cut off his escape in every direction, except by means of the shore toward which all were so rapidly hastening.

"It is a useless waste of strength," said the pursued. 'I've hunted too long along the banks of this river to run into any trap of your invention. You might put your muscles to better use than attempting to catch me."

A moment later he had entered the shadows on the southern shore. Running down-stream a short distance, he forced his canoe in to land. Then springing ashore, he struck off into the wood, on his usual deliberate walk.

"P'raps the canoe might have been kept out of thar hands, but, as it ain't likely I'll need it, except to cross in the morning, which can easily be done without it, it ain't worth the trouble. They're welcome to it and all the good it will ever do them."

He pursued his way, occasionally pausing to listen for signs of pursuit; but, correctly supposing none would be attempted, he gave himself little trouble on that ground. Still, he journeyed forward for a considerable length of time, when he reached a small hollow-like depression, removed from the river-bank, and sheltered by exuberant vegetation. Here, by means of his spark and tinder, he kindled a small fire of twigs and partially dried branches. It burned but poorly, and gave little or no warmth; he wished it for a different purpose. As soon as the thin, fan-like blaze ascended, he took the small piece of shingle, or board, which had been handed him by Musconondon. The light was so faint and uncertain, and he had so disfigured it by carrying it as the Indian did, in his mouth, that the writing had been well-nigh obliterated. He recognized the bold, handsome writing, however, and after a while traced out the following words:

"To FOREST SPY:—Tecumseh, it is now certain, is in the South, stirring up the Indians in that section. Those in the North have already been incited to that point that a bloody war is inevitable. Watch him; follow him, and let no movement of his escape you. Report yourself to me as soon as it can be done. I send this by Musconondon, who must return as soon as it is delivered. You need return nothing, as his word is all-sufficient. W. H. H."

"I'll sleep on that, I guess," said the Spy, laying it under his head, as if it were a pillow, and almost immediately dropping off in slumber.

## CHAPTER IV.

### THE PROGRESS OF EVENTS.

This is the strangest fellow, brother John.
KING HENRY IV.

There is more news:
I learned in Worcester, as I rode along.
He can not draw his power this fourteen days.
IBID.

THE Forest Spy slept soundly until the rays of the morning sun stole through the tree-branches, when his every sense appeared to awake at the same moment. He arose to his feet, read the writing upon the chip once more, and then walked off in a direction that led him both down and toward the river, apparently regardless of the wants of nature which were making themselves felt. When he reached the bank, he went still further down the stream, all the while scrutinizing the opposite shore, with his usual closeness and care. Satisfied with the appearance, he rolled a large section of a rotten tree, that lay along the bank, into the water. Slinging his rifle over his back, he straddled the log, and commenced paddling himself across by means of an extemporized paddle.

His progress was necessarily slow, and when he touched the opposite side, it was a quarter of a mile lower, and fully a half-hour later. While his head was bent, and seemingly occupied entirely with his efforts to move the awkward structure through the water, his eyes were never once removed from the wood that lined the other shore, and, after twenty years' life in the forest, it was not probable that he would commit a fatal mistake in such a simple act as crossing the river. When he landed, therefore, he stepped upon the bank with a self-confident air, and moved off as though no thought of danger had ever entered his mind.

A quarter of a mile distant from the river, he struck a sort of road, unfenced on either side, but which had a deep rut half covered with grass, as if a settler's wagon had passed that way some time before. In the center of this road was a winding path, which Forest Spy followed with the greatest caution, as he had no desire to encounter strangers in that section. The road was very winding, and in turning one of the corners, he saw a man spring from it into the wood. He instantly did the same,

when the stranger sprung back to view again, showing himself
to be a white hunter.

"Hello! show yourself!" he shouted, in a voice that might
be heard a mile away.

Forest Spy did so, and saw a man before him rather below
the medium stature, thick-set, with long black hair, rather prepossessing features, and an air and expression of perfect recklessness. There was a frank, candid look in his face, mingled
with the most imperturbable good-humor.

"What's the news?" he demanded, in the same vociferous
tone, as he reached out to take the proffered hand.

"I suppose you've heard that Tecumseh has been, or for that
matter, is still in these parts, stirring up the Creeks against the
whites."

"No, I hadn't heard nothing," replied the stranger, without
abating the loudness of his tone in the least.

"I think if Tecumseh is in the Creek country, he'll hear you,
if you don't lower that voice of yourn, now."

"Pshaw, now! get out! Say, you," said the loud-voiced,
good-natured stranger, with a shrewd twinkle of his eye, folding his arms and striking them over the muzzle of his rifle, and
twisting his right foot around the other leg so that it rested
on its toe: "Say, you, where might that roaring Tecumseh be
just now?"

"Not many miles distant, though I couldn't exactly name the
place."

"S'posen you and I go into partnership, eh? Let's splice
and capture him, and take him on to Washington for a show.
It'll make a time among them Congress fellers. What say?"

"You would make a name that would never die, if you could
secure that chief; but it's a job that can never be done by a
white or red-man."

"I don't know about that," replied the stranger, speaking for
the first time in a somewhat lower tone. "I don't know about
that. I've throwed many a b'ar in my time, and I wouldn't be
afraid of a set-to with him. I hear he's great on making speeches, and, as I've some idea of doing that same thing, one reason I
want to catch him, is to stop that."

'Wal, my friend, I hope you will succeed, but I'm afraid you
never will. I don't believe there's any use of my going with
you; so I'll let you share the great honor alone."

"All right, stranger; when you hear Tecumseh has been
cotched, you'll feel sorry that you can't claim part of the honor.
If the old chieftain stays in these parts long enough, I'll catch
him, sure."

"Is that what you started for?"

"Not exactly; the old woman and the little ones at home

are getting rather short of meat; so I've been out for b'ars and venzon."

"What luck?"

"Wal, tol'able. P'raps you heerd Betsy here bark awhile ago? Didn't eh? I hain't brought down no deer yet; but in the way of b'ars, I fotched a regular screamer a mile or two back—enough to keep the mouths a-goin' for nigh on to a month."

"I must go on, friend, if you are not going my way."

"No; I've keeled a varmint over, and I'm going after that varmint of a Tecumseh. When I catch him, he must promise to stop making *speeches*, or I'll duck him in the river and then drown him. Good-by!" he yelled, striking up a whistle and starting off on a free and easy walk. "Say, you, hello!" he shouted, wheeling suddenly around, after he had walked a rod or so.

"Well, what is wanted?" asked the Forest Spy, rather impatiently.

"What moght chance to be your handle, eh? No 'bjections, I s'pose?"

"I'm called the Forest Spy, where I'm known."

"Queer name, that! b'lieve I've heard of you—quite a hunter. Good-by—hello again! Do you know me?"

"I don't know as I do; I believe I have never met you."

"I know that, or you'd remember me. I'm known in these parts as Davy Crockett, the b'ar hunter. Good-by!"

And whistling merrily, the eccentric but remarkable man disappeared around a curve in the road.

"He may be Davy Crockett the bear hunter," mused the Spy, as he moved slowly along. "But he's got a good deal to learn yet about hunting Indians. Going to catch Tecumseh! Ah's me, such a feller would look better in Congress than anywhere else. He surely must have been jesting, or else is underwitted."

The speaker pursued his way for over a mile further, when the wood became more open, and he arrived opposite a cabin, which stood about a hundred yards from the road. Here he stepped behind a tree, and gave the same signal that he had upon approaching the clearing the night before. He had hardly uttered it, when the door partly opened and a man's head appeared, and was seen to look around as if to determine from what direction it had come. The Forest Spy repeated it, and the face was instantly turned toward him, and an answer sent back. This seemed to satisfy him, for he stepped from his concealment, and in a few moments was admitted into the settler's cabin.

Within the house were a short, fat, dwarfish half-breed, with a broad, expressionless face, and his wife, a well-formed, handsome Creek woman. The former was very talkative, and was a perfect contrast in features, mind and temperament to the hunter, whom he denominated "Spy."

"Well, Spy," said he, seating himself and his friend at the same moment, with a great show and ceremony, "Well, Spy, the war has about commenced."

"Yes; it seems idle to hope to defer it any longer."

"Just so, exactly; just what I've said these ten years. Tecumseh's the man to do it, too. That chief is a terrible man; I never heard such a speech as he made last night. You ought to have heard him, Spy—"

"I did," quietly interrupted the hunter.

"Wasn't it awful—tremenjous—cavortin—grand? I tell you what, it stirred the blood in *me*. If it wasn't for two or three things, I'd dig up the hatchet, I b'lieve."

"What might those things be?"

"The first is I am constitutionally opposed to fighting—have always done what I could against it; and then, you see, my family is sort of divided. Molly, my wife there, is a Creek, while I'm half-Creek and half-American; and, to be honest, if I should fight, I must fight on both sides. Ha! ha! ha! And I'm in too dangerous territories to try *that* trick. You see I may be said to be on the dividing line, and both parties will occasionally stop at my house; so I've concluded to be friendly to any one who stops, making him believe, at the same time, that I lean toward his side. Ha! ha! ha! Bright idea, Spy?"

"*Safe*, I suppose."

"Must be; but what are you driving at, Spy? This is the first time I've heard your call in these parts for many a day, and I could hardly believe it was you, 'though I knowed no other hunter ever originated such a signal. Good idea, Spy; ha! ha! ha!"

"I've been through the Creek country, to see what success Tecumseh is going to have. I s'pose you know and will not refuse to tell me?"

"Of course not; for you see, I've a leaning toward your side," said the half-breed, with a leer and twinkle. Then putting on a more serious air, he added: "the Creeks are going to dig up the hatchet, *but not right away*. Tecumseh has been among the Seminoles and didn't succeed in stirring all their chiefs up with his tremendous eloquence. The Creeks know that, and they will hold back *for a while*; but, depend upon it, it won't be long—not more than two weeks at the most, before they'll be hacking and cutting, and robbing cabins and carrying off females—"

"They are doing it already," quietly interrupted the hunter.
"What do you mean, Spy?"
"Gorman Lindower and his sister."
"Ah, yes! I know what you mean; but that wasn't the Creeks; they helped to carry it out, but they didn't plan it, nor do it alone."
"Who planned it? The Shawnees?"
"No; the Shawnee."
"Who do you mean?"
"Tecumseh," replied the breed, in a whisper, and glancing furtively around, as if afraid the walls might hear that name.
"What?" demanded the Forest Spy, springing to his feet, as if struck with a dagger, and betraying the most extraordinary excitement.
"Why, bless my soul? What's the matter, Spy? I don't see any thing alarming in that—not at all. I'd rather have Tecumseh do it than any one else; for you know he's trying to stop that barbarous habit of burning prisoners among his people, and as long as he has them they're safe."
"I know," replied the hunter, as if musing with himself. "But, do you know when Tecumseh leaves?"
"I expect he is on his way this minute—"
"I must be off then; for I must get north as soon as he does."
"You can do it if anybody can, Spy," said the half-breed, rising as his visitor did. "There's no need cautioning you to be careful. You know I should hate to have you lost, as my sympathies are with your side entirely," he added, with another twinkle. "There's Davy Crockett, a great hunter, a very clever fellow, and a good friend of mine, but one I'm desperately afraid for. He's crossed the river into the Creek country, knowing that we—I mean they are tremendous mad just now and very dangerous."
"I met him just now, and can say that he's very careless; but the Lord seems to take care of such chaps."
"What I've always said. Me and Crockett were out hunting one day, and got belated in a swamp. It was so tremendous cold that we tried to start a fire—"

The half-breed ceased, for the Forest Spy was already beyond his hearing, moving forward with unusually long, rapid strides—a sure evidence that he was excited by something unusual. Now and then he muttered brokenly to himself, and when alone in the wood, where but One could see and hear him, he suddenly halted, and, striking his rifle down with a rattling clamp up on the ground, as he slowly shook his head from side to side, said:

"It's what I feared, it's what I feared. If the Creeks had done it, or even the Shawnees, it wouldn't look so dark, for I've been many a time with the villains, and could have managed the matter *in time;* but the way it is, it's the hardest job I ever looked upon. As I'm serving the Gineral, I shall be busy enough; but this *heart-business.*" The speaker paused a moment, as if struck with the sound of the last words. "Yes, it's *heart-business* for me, and this must be carried out. To serve the Gineral and myself requires that I should move to the northward, and I but lose time in these foolish talkings."

Once more he hurried away, and before the sun disappeared behind the western forest, he was many leagues from the half-breed's cabin.

On the twelfth day, the Forest Spy appeared before the American encampment at Tippecanoe. It was late in the autumn, two days after that celebrated battle had taken place. His observations during the journey had made him certain that some desperate engagement had lately taken place. He had passed by the prophet's town, and saw that it was deserted, and had discovered evidences of the hurried retreat of a large body of Indians. When he emerged into the plain of Tippecanoe, and saw his countrymen engaged in burying their fallen companions, he was satisfied that the engagement had been desperate and sanguinary.

Giving the countersign to different sentinels, several of whom were old acquaintances, he was ushered into the presence of the commanding officer. The General, at the time, was engaged in writing, and did not look up as his visitor was announced. The Forest Spy coolly seated himself, and occupied the time in gazing about the tent and in watching the quill as it nodded backward and forward, and scratched rapidly over the paper. In a few moments he dashed the sand upon it, wheeled around, and spoke:

"Ah! so you have arrived. I am very glad to see you. Did Musconondon give you my message?"

"He did, Gineral," replied the hunter, respectfully, "and your orders were obeyed."

"You need not tell me that; for I have long known that your will never conflicts with duty. You are esteemed an honest and invaluable soldier by me."

A glow of pleasure passed over the weather-beaten face of the hunter, and he stammered something unintelligible to the General, who kindly relieved him:

"You have seen Tecumseh, of course?"

"Yes, Gineral; I heard his speech to the Creeks."

"What effect had it? Was it a stirring one?"

"It was awful—*terrible!*" exclaimed the hunter, gesticulating awkwardly. "I set in a tree-top and held on till he got purty near through, when I dropped to the ground and run—for, Gineral, *I couldn't stand it!*"

A pleasant smile crossed the face of the commander, but quickly disappeared as he asked:

"And what effect had it upon the Creeks? Did they run, too?"

"Oh, heavens! they got so mad and excited, that they was ready to tear each other to pieces. Just before I jumped down I took a look at them. Their eyes shone so I do believe I could have lit my pipe by them; and the way their breasts heaved and sunk, and the way the wind come between their teeth, I do think would have filled the sails of a frigate. Oh, it was terrible, Gineral."

The recollections of the speech, it was evident, were strong and vivid thus to excite the hunter. The General, without heeding this awkward enthusiasm, asked:

"What more did you learn regarding Tecumseh?"

"Well, I staid till he and his chiefs started north again, and it wasn't long either. I talked with a half-breed, who'd heard his speech, and who is an acquaintance of mine. He told me the Creeks would fight sure, though they might not commence right away."

"I have no doubt they, as well as the other tribes in that section, will dig up the hatchet. It will make warm work for Jackson, and the others in that part of the country; but I have no fears of the result. I interrupt you, however."

"Well, I got on the track of the chiefs at last, and followed them through Missouri, among the tribes of the Des Moines; seen them cross the head-waters of the Illinois, and at last reach the Wabash, where I left them. Everywhere Tecumseh was speechifying to them."

"With great success, I suppose?"

"When white nature can't stand Tecumseh's eloquence, you may set it down as onpossible for Injin nature to do it. There's no calculating the deviltry that fellow has set afoot. He has started a fire burning that will go like the flame on the prairie. This is all I l'arnt, and I conclude you wil' agree 'tis plenty. But, Gineral, you've had a brush while the old chief was gone."

"We have; and, although it has made many a brave fellow bite the dust, I can but believe it was one of the most fortunate things that could have happened for our arms. I have learned from Musconondon that Tecumseh left positive orders for his followers to keep peace with us until his return; but they were persuaded into the battle by his brother, the prophet, who made them believe they could annihilate me without the loss of one of their number, whereas their defeat has been disastrous, and the slaughter terrible. So enraged are they at the prophet, that his life is really in danger, and his power is completely broken. Another great result is that this formidable confederacy which Tecumseh has brought about, will be dissolved by this battle."

"I trust so, Gineral; but it looks mighty onsartain."

"On the contrary, it is certain. The Kickapoos are encamped but a short distance away; the Pottawatomies have scattered and returned to their village; and scarcely a Winnebago is to be seen. All these tribes have suffered severe losses in this battle, and are so exasperated at the prophet that Tecumseh's eloquence can never bring them back into the confederacy again."

"I'm rejoiced to hear it; but, Gineral, there's been reports circulating for some time back about a war with the red-coats. Be the reports idle, or have they foundation?"

"I'm sorry to say that a war with England is inevitable. We shall have our hands full of fighting in a year or so."

"Where will Tecumseh and the other devils be then?"

"With the British, most certainly; and we shall have as bloody a fighting-ground with the savages as the continent will see during the entire war."

"That's a fact, Gineral, that's a fact; they'll make up for these defeats they've suffered with a vengeance; but, if my eyes sarve me right, you haven't come out of the battle unhurt."

"To what do you refer?" asked the officer, with some surprise.

"I see a red spot on your neck, as if made by a bullet."

"Oh! that is what you mean!" laughed the commander, good-naturedly. "Yes, a bullet passed through my stock, and bruised my neck a little—very little."

"No other hurt?"

"One in the thigh—not worth mentioning."

"Nothing else?" persisted the hunter.

"Nothing else my good friend, except that my horse was killed under me. But you seem unusually interested in my welfare."

"Not more than I always am, Gineral. I hope I'll never live to see you die. But you was talking about the war with England. How soon will it commence?"

"It's uncertain; in a few months, I should suppose."

"Till that time there will be peace, p'raps, in these parts?"

"Yes; the confederation being broken up, I feel certain of no further trouble from these savages until they take sides with England."

"Will I be needed by you before that time, Gineral?"

"Most assuredly, my friend; I can never think of dispensing

with your services before the war has ended. I shall want you to watch the movements of Tecumseh and his followers continually, and detect the first signs of an uprising among them. We never needed you more than we do at this time."

A slight shade of disappointment crossed the features of the Spy—so slight that General Harrison failed to notice it. He entertained not the slightest suspicion that there could be any other thoughts than those of service in the mind of his servant, and he consequently failed to look for them. The hunter himself had several times been on the point of asking leave of him to engage upon a sort of private expedition—one which has been vaguely hinted at in the preceding pages; but a fear of betraying the part his own feelings took in the matter prevented him. Several times he actually commenced the question, but broke down each time. Nothing seemed so humiliating to him as to be suspected, at his age, of being guilty of a weakness more often seen in men of more youthful blood than his own. The kind-hearted commander endeavored to disembarrass him, and draw out the troublesome communication but failed; and the interview terminated, for the first time, to the dissatisfaction of the faithful Forest Spy.

## CHAPTER V.

### THE TWO HUNTERS.

*Yet am I arm'd against the worst can happen;
And haste is needful in this desperate case.*
       KING HENRY VI.

Two years have passed since the events recorded in the preceding pages, and it is again autumn. A mild, hazy afternoon is drawing to a close, with all the delicious silence and coolness so characteristic of an American forest. The soft, almost inaudible breath of the woods is undisturbed by the cry of its numerous denizens. Every thing is wooed by repose. Overhead the deep blue sky is flecked by a few small clouds, drifting like snow flakes through the clear air. The sullen wash of Lake Erie upon its sandy shore, gives a monotonous dreaminess to the scene, and it would have required no great effort of the imagination for the dweller in these parts to imagine himself in a country as yet undiscovered by civilized man.

On a small eminence, a few rods from the lake, were seated, upon the afternoon in question, two men in the garb of hunters. At the moment we introduce them, they were engaged in eating a turkey, cooked at a fire now smoldering at their side. A tree with low-falling branches protected them from observation, while their view of the lake was almost unobstructed.

The two men were the Forest Spy and Gorman Lindower. Their most intimate acquaintance would have failed to recognize them—so completely were they disguised. The face of the former was stained until its color was as swarthy as that of an Indian, while his hair was of a yellowish, sandy hue. His dress, however, was precisely similar to what already has been described. The hair of Lindower—naturally of a light color—was now a deep black, while his face also resembled tarnished copper. The legs of the Forest Spy were bent under him, similar to a tailor when at work, while "Spitfire" was balanced across his knees. His hands were grasping the ends of bone, from which he was wrenching off a mouthful of the delicious flesh. When the rich, oozing juice rendered his grasp uncertain, he hurriedly drew his hands through his hair, and returned to the work more vigorously than ever.

Although in disguise, there was a perceptible difference between the two. Gorman Lindower was fully ten years younger than the Spy, rather below the medium size, with a powerfully developed frame, and a naturally florid countenance, upon which, for a long time, there had rested a settled expression of melancholy. He was taciturn and thoughtful, and generally replied to his somewhat more talkative companion with a monosyllable, or, at times, with a simple grunt. Instead of wearing the close-fitting fur-cap of the Forest Spy, his head-gear consisted of a slouched beaver, manufactured in the "settlements," which set off his face to good advantage. In other respects the dress of the two was the same.

"To get the right taste of a critter like this, I'm thinkin', Gorman, a man must fast a good night and day as we have. How does it suit?"

An approving grunt was the only reply, uttered with a mouth full and jaws moving rapidly.

"Knowing your consaits and ideas, I take that answer as it is meant, Gorman, which is that your stomach does not revolt at the stuff. I'm rejoiced that your appetite still remains, as it shows you're not frightened at the risk before us."

"Ugh?" questioned Lindower, suddenly closing his mouth over a bone, and looking inquiringly into the face of the Spy.

"I was only saying," replied the latter, with a sigh of pleasure as he cleaned his fingers upon his hair, and looked around to decide the next place of attack upon the food. "I was only saying that I'm glad to see you're not frightened at the job before us, for it's one that needs a cool head."

"S'pose'll have time to finish it?" asked Lindower, hurriedly still moving his jaws with great rapidity.

"I've no fear, Gorman. Finding that the Gineral was of the idee I ought to be busy all the time, I come down with the question, whether he couldn't spare me and you for a few weeks. When I told him the circumstances of Laura's mishap, and how I had waited two years hoping the time would come when we might strike a blow for her, he told me I should go at once, and said, I should have had his consent two years ago if I had only asked it. I take some blame to heart that I did wait so long."

For a few minutes, nothing but the munching of teeth was heard, as the two men continued their work. The turkey was rapidly diminishing before their keen appetites, and had soon dwindled to a few bones. Then both ceased, the Spy replaced his cap upon his head, and rising to his feet, said:

"The sun is well down in the sky, Gorman, and Tecumseh's encampment is a long tramp away. It's your wish to reach it to night, I b'lieve."

"Yeh."

"We must be on the move then, for, in a few hours more, night will be upon us."

The Spy struck into his long and noiseless strides, followed by Lindower, whose steps were shorter and necessarily quicker. Now and then the former made some remark to which the latter replied with his usual grunt—the answer seeming perfectly intelligible and satisfactory to the leader. In this manner they advanced for a couple of hours or more, by which time the sun had entirely disappeared, and the gloom of night was closing rapidly around them.

The reader has probably suspected the errand of these two hunters. In a preceding chapter we have shown how one of them, with his sister Laura, was deprived of his home by a band of Indians. The two had not seen each other since the night of their capture, but, about a year previous, Gorman Lindower had succeeded in effecting his escape, and had spent the subsequent time in searching for his sister, though without success, until within a few days, when Nockwynee, now a friendly Indian, brought him intelligence that a white woman was a prisoner of Tecumseh's. At the time we introduce him he had been several days on his journey and was now within a short distance of the Shawnee encampment.

Years before, when Lindower and his sister lived near the settlements, and when she was quite a woman, the Forest Spy had visited their section, and remained for several years. Little was known of him more than that he came from Kentucky, where he had been engaged in the numerous Indian war along the frontier. The time of his visit was several years after the opening of the present century, and was occasioned, it was believed, by the period of peace which was then reigning. The parents of Lindower died nearly at the same time, and he and his sister were left alone in the world. Shortly after, their acquaintance with the Spy commenced, and it was evident that he looked upon Laura Lindower with more than ordinary regard. He visited the brother and sister often, and showed his attachment in many quaint and singular ways. It is uncertain when matters would have arrived at a culminating point, as, after years of courtship—if the term is allowable in this case—the actions and words of the lover were precisely the same. Laura Lindower, at this time, had long been out of her teens. She received the characteristic attentions of her old suitor as if she perfectly understood them, and was content to wait the progress of events. At the end of several years, Gorman formed the determination to migrate into that rich country inhabited by the Creek Indians. Forest Spy opposed this scheme with great earnestness, pointing out the danger that was growing more and more apparent every day; but, one element in the brother's character was a dogged determination that would not be turned from its purpose. The evening previous to their departure Laura noticed the confusion and embarrassment of her lover. He was as confused and awkward as a boy. She endeavored to place him at his ease, but at the critical moment, a messenger arrived with a notice from General Harrison for the Spy. It would admit of no delay, and he took his departure the same hour. He went north, where he remained in the service of the General for two years, when he was sent south to watch the motions of the Creeks, and of the chief, Tecumseh. This visit we have taken occasion to describe in our first chapter. We have shown how he visited the house of Lindower and found it rifled of its contents, and was satisfied that its inmates were prisoners. It was his earnest wish to engage in a search for them, but his obligations prevented him. He was high in the confidence of General Harrison and was intrusted with weighty and important matters, from which he could not shrink. In his character of spy upon the disaffected Indians, he was afforded considerable opportunity for observation and question regarding the captured brother and sister, but he was rewarded with no success. At this time there were scores of white people in the hands of the confederate tribe, and being restrained by his duty to his country, the way to success in the discovery and release of his friends may be said to have been blocked up.

A year previous, as has been mentioned, Gorman effected his escape, and met the Spy. The brother, although very anxious in regard to his sister, still was hopeful of her final recovery. He knew the chivalrous feelings which actuated Tecumseh, and knowing, too, that she was held by him, was satisfied no harm would be offered her. But this latter fact seemed to annoy the Spy more than any thing else. His agitation upon learning the truth from the half-breed, and the many dark hints he had dropped to the brother, showed that he had disagreeable suspicions. There was certainly some mystery which he was unwilling to reveal, but which was a source of continual torment to him. So great became his anxiety that, at length, he went to Harrison and stated frankly the case, and asked a furlough of several weeks' duration that he might be at liberty to prosecute the search. The commander granted his wish without a moment's hesitation, and, with a commendable kindness, inquired into his plans for rescuing the captive in case he should discover her situation. The Spy replied that he had not settled upon any plan, but had proposed to Gorman to reconnoiter the camp, and, in case his sister were seen, to enter it in disguise, as he had done on several occasions. The danger of attempting this was such (especially as his doings of late had rendered him notorious among the Indians) that the General gave him a message to Tecumseh, under pretext of which he might enter the Indian encampment without fear of molestation. Instead of disguising himself as an Indian—as was his first intention—at the suggestion of Harrison himself, he concluded to color his hair and stain his face in such a manner that, while he would naturally be taken for a white man, no one would suspect his identity. Supposing him to be only an ordinary messenger, he would attract little attention, and, as he believed, be allowed the chance of observing the appearance of matters around him. Failing in this, he was to enter the camp as the Indian of another tribe, in which character he was confident he could accomplish all that he desired.

With these explanations the actions of the two hunters will be better understood.

---

Forest Spy maintained his long, noiseless strides, always keeping beside the river, until in the darkness they resembled shadows moving through the forest. They kept up the journey without conversation until near midnight, when the full moon had risen above them. As they were crossing an open patch in the woods, the Spy suddenly faced around toward his companion, and removing his cap, asked:

"What do I look like, Gorman?"

"Humph!—anybody but yourself."

"Does this yellow on my hair look natural?"

"Humph."

"And this yeller beard and stains on my face—are they all right?"

"Humph."

"I'm glad to hear it, for, Gorman, it would be *slightly* dangerous for Tecumseh to find us out. You're disguised up so, there's none there who'd suspect you were a prisoner among 'em a year ago; but, being it was another tribe who held you, 'tain't likely you'd run any danger even if you hadn't painted your hair and face. But, we're upon the encampment now and must go forward. Remember, Gorman, I'm the embassador from the Gineral, and will have all the talking to do. You must have nothing to say."

"S'posen they find us out, eh?"

"I don't think they will; but in case they do, *you* will still be safe. Tecumseh will allow you to go, though he will take the trouble, like enough, to keep me."

"What makes you so 'fraid of Tecumseh?" questioned Lindower, prompted to this unusual flow of language only by his great curiosity.

"You will know, some day, Gorman. I haven't the time to explain now. Let us go on."

With this, the two moved forward again. Scarce a hundred yards were passed, when they once more emerged from the wood into a vast open space dotted by the numerous wigwams of the Indian village. Numerous forms were visible, and before they had advanced a dozen steps they were approached by several sentinels. Forest Spy waved his hand for them to make way, muttering at the same time the name of Tecumseh. They seemed to divine that he and his companion were messengers. Two Indians walked in front as if to conduct them into the presence of their chief. The village was laid out somewhat after the manner of streets. After going quite a distance through what seemed the main avenue, the two Indians halted before a large and tastefully-arranged lodge. Motioning for the two strangers to follow, they pulled a blanket aside and entered. This act afforded a momentary view of the interior, when Forest Spy saw with alarm that a number of British officers were present. Had he suspected this, nothing would have induced him to enter the precincts of the Indian village, as he well feared the efficiency of *any* disguise in the presence of such enemies. It was now too late, however, and without evincing the least hesitation, he entered the apartment. He saw that he was in a council. With his knowledge of Indian custom, he seated himself without noticing any one, Lindower doing the same.

For the space of ten minutes our two friends sat perfectly

motionless, during which time not a syllable was uttered by any one present. Both felt that every eye was fixed upon them. They bore the ordeal manfully. The pipe was then produced and passed to Gorman. He took a few whiffs, then handed it to his companion, who in turn passed it to the Indian nearest him. After it had completed the circuit of the room, Forest Spy arose, knowing that the time had approached when he was expected to make his message known.

"Brothers, the Chief of Seventeen Fires desires to be on good terms with his Indian brethren. He is willing to pardon and forget what you have done in the past, provided you cease hostile acts in the future.

"Brothers, our chief wishes you good. The war has gone on for two years without benefit to your cause. Should not this teach you that it is useless to resist the American people? Should you not be willing to make peace with them?

"Brothers, we wish to smoke the calumet of peace with you."

Having finished, Forest Spy resumed his posture in such a manner that his gaze was fixed upon no one. It is generally the custom, when a speech is made in Indian council, for the reply to be deferred until the next day; but, exceptions sometimes occur, and Forest Spy knew the present occasion would be one. Accordingly, when the time which savage decorum requires had elapsed, Tecumseh sprung to his feet, and, with startling voice and excited gesture, gave his reply:

"Does your chief suppose Tecumseh a dog? Does he seek to trample upon him as upon the snake? Does he send men to sing lying words in his ears, that he may be soothed and turned aside?

"Tecumseh asks no peace of the white man. He is strong enough to fight his own battles. His arm shall be raised against the Americans forever. He tears the words you have uttered from his ears. He seeks the scalp of your General and of the great Father at Washington. Tell them what has been said. Tecumseh has spoken."

This emphatic reply took neither of our friends by surprise. They well knew what to expect from the Shawnee leader. Speeches and peace-offerings had long been exhausted with him. Had the latter been offered with any degree of seriousness, it would have been the merest folly. As has been hinted, our friends were exercising a little generalship, with a personal object. They were, therefore, prepared for the reply of the exasperated Indian. Nevertheless, Forest Spy deemed it prudent to manifest considerable surprise, and his answer was, simply:

"Brothers, we will carry your words to our chief," making

a movement as if to depart; when several of the officers whispered together, and Tecumseh instantly added:

"The path to my brother chieftain's camp is long and full of turnings. His messenger will await the rising of the sun before venturing on it."

"The path is well beaten and free of briers. Our Gineral's messengers can travel it in the night as well as in the day," replied Forest Spy, gradually approaching the door. He noticed another exchange of significant looks and whispers between the British officers, when Tecumseh replied, with considerable emphasis:

"The white men will stay in the lodges of Tecumseh's people this night."

This declaration, equivalent to a positive command, was heard by the adventurers with well-grounded alarm. Despite his disguise, the Spy firmly believed his true character was suspected by the officers, among whom he noticed Proctor himself. His identity once discovered, he felt there was little hope; he was not ignorant of the penalty attached to the name of spy. Besides, he knew Proctor had long since offered a reward for his apprehension; while still further, there was a matter unsettled between himself and Tecumseh, which had forever closed the door of mercy to him. He was too prudent, however, to manifest any uneasiness, knowing there was but one course left, and remained waiting until he should be conducted away. In a moment, the skin which hung as a door was pulled aside, and the two Indians who had conducted them thither now signified that they should again follow.

The guides led the way through the narrow, gloomy path, or street, for a short distance, when they suddenly turned aside and entered another lodge, perfectly dark.

"Stay here," was the laconic command of the guides.

The opening through which they had entered closed, and our two friends were alone in the apartment. Feeling around for a while, they gathered some idea of its shape and size. There were mats or skins beneath them, and as they really were exhausted, they lay down. They had lain thus but a moment when Lindower abruptly asked:

"Say, can't we get out of this?"

His companion turned over on his side so as to face the speaker, and waiting a moment, as though he were looking him full in the face, replied:

"There's no denying that I have found affairs considerably different from what I expected. I had no idea them British officers, and especially that Proctor, were in *these* parts. I've little fear for *you*; but, if I get out of these parts without considerable questioning, I shall be mightily mistaken."

"Let's tear out and run."

"Put your ears to the ground a minute, Gorman, and listen."

Both did so, and heard distinctly the regular tramp of feet.

"That," said the Spy, in a husky whisper, "you know is made by Indian moccasins. There are a dozen tramping around this lodge, and they will do so until morning. I'm much afraid we'll have to wait till morning."

"I won't."

"Eh! how's that?"

"I tell you my chance will be as bad as yours. I had to wipe out a Shawnee before I could get off last summer, and they've never forgot it. If they suspect you, they'll suspect me. I'm going to make a dash out of here, and that mighty soon too."

Lindower, when excited, was as talkative as his companion. He continued muttering and threatening to himself, while the Spy lay still, ruminating deeply upon what he had just seen and heard. All hope of finding out any thing of the object of his visit was now given over. It had been his intention to propound the question to Tecumseh himself, during the council, but the presence of his country's enemies had not only prevented it, but, as we have stated, had given him some idea of the risk he ran in thus entering a hostile Indian village upon the eve of a great battle.

This latter fact, however, for reasons which will hereafter be seen, was the real cause of his visit being made at this particular time.

The Spy, pondering deeply, finally, in answer to the mutterings of his companion, said:

"Gorman, you noticed that officer who was next to Tecumseh?"

"Yeah; I b'lieve I've seen him somewhere before."

"That's what struck me when I sot eyes on him first. I've been thinking who he was, and have just found out. You remember that deserter who come into our camp, a few days after you did, and who turned up missing a week after?"

"Ah! yes, he's the feller."

"He's the man. He came in as a deserter when he was a spy, and when he left, went back to the enemy. Gorman, that man seen both of us that time, and he knew us both to-night."

"Then what in blazes are we stretched out here for?" demanded Lindower, coming to the upright position and indignantly facing the Spy.

"Hush! hush! you're too loud, you're too excited, Gorman. They'll hear you on the outside, and all will be done for. Just listen to me. That fellow has told Tecumseh who we are, and he'll pass sentence on us both as spies, and will execute us as such. My speech was too flimsy to hide our real motive. Consequently, we must try and get out of here to-night."

"Give me your hand on that, old feller," exclaimed the impetuous Lindower.

"There's little need of shaking hands," replied the Spy, doing it, however, while he was speaking. "It's plain the thing has got to be done, and we must make ready. It can't be far from midnight, and so we'll commence. You keep still now. Gorman, and let me take an observation."

The Spy arose and commenced a stealthy examination of the lodge. Several times he passed entirely around the interior so noiselessly that even Lindower could not detect his footsteps, although those upon the outside were audible all the time.

"It's nothing but a common Indian lodge," said he, reseating himself. "As near as I can calculate we're about in the center of the village, which makes it rather bad when the run is to be made."

"But how are we going to get out?" impatiently demanded Lindower.

"You're too excited, you're too excited. Depend upon it, Gorman, you'll spoil all. I find the door of this lodge is a buffalo-skin. I drawed my knife across the upper part, so that a twitch will pull the whole thing out of the way. I took a peep, and seen the villains all around, some standing still, while a head about every second went past the door, it being them that you hear walking around us. Now, the question is whether we shall make a rush out of the back part or out of the front, or one of us take the back and the other the front."

"Any way, so we *get out.*"

"Just so. My idee, then, is for me to take the buffalo-skin and you the back part. We'll soon cut a way for you. We'll make the dash at the same minute, and one, any way, will stand a chance of getting off if he uses his pegs as he ought to."

"Which one?"

"That can't be told, Gorman. Every part of this wigwam is watched. There may be more in front of it than behind it. If they think we will make the trial—and they probably do—they may keep a closer eye on every part than the rig'lar entrance. Howsumever, as I just said, the matter is desperately onsartain."

The matter was by no means uncertain, and the Spy well knew he was giving the chance to his companion. He saw how closely the entrance was watched. He had resolved in his own mind to rush from the door before Lindower could make his escape, and by thus drawing pursuit upon himself, afford him a better opportunity to make off.

What rendered this scheme doubly desperate, was the aright

moonlight that prevailed. Had the Spy been in the disguise of an Indian, he was confident that, by doubling around the lodges and mixing in with the savages themselves, he could effect his own escape. As it was, he was fully sensible of the almost utter hopelessness of the trial he was about to make.

But, the matter being decided, they set about putting it into execution at once. The lodge was composed simply of skins and bark—constructed, of course, without the intention of using it as a prison. The Spy, on his hands and knees, drew his knife carefully and skillfully along the side, cutting the bark and skin clean through in several places, and rendering it so weak in other parts that a slight pressure would force out a large, square piece, amply sufficient to permit the passage of a man. So great was the caution used in doing this, that a full half hour elapsed before the operator announced that "all was ready." During this time, Lindower was in such a fever of impatience as to be barely able to restrain himself; but, now that the moment of action had come, he suddenly became as cool and collected as the Spy himself.

"Keep cool," admonished the latter; "take your station, Gorman, and let me guide your hand over the crease I have made, so that you'll understand exactly how to work."

This was done, and the Spy approached the door, where he was to make his own attempt.

"Now," said he, "be sure and wait till you see moonlight here, and then—"

"Yes, I will."

A crash drowned the rest of the sentence. The impetuous Lindower bolted through the opening, as much to the surprise of his friend as of his enemies. As quick as thought, the former jerked the buffalo-robe from its place, and, with a defiant yell, bounded outward, overturning two Indians, and fleeing directly through the village at the top of his speed.

The reckless Lindower executed a more successful maneuver than his debut seemed to promise. Turning sharply off to his right, ducking his head, and dodging from right to left so as to escape the shots of his enemies, he succeeded in placing several wigwams between them and himself. In fact, it might not be an inapt figure to compare his movements to a flash of lightning, so zigzag, swift and erratic were they. The flight and yell of his friend at the same moment greatly aided him—in fact, insured his safety. He made no noise, but kept running, dodging, and whirling around the lodges, taking a direction at right angles to the Spy's, who at that moment was flying, yelling, down the main street, pursued by a horde of savages. Now and then a form sprung up and confronted Lindower, but his tremendous gait soon left all behind, or the force of his descending rifle hushed the savage forever. On he sped, winding and turning, dodging and avoiding encounters, never ceasing his terrific efforts, until at length he burst into the woods amid the shots of a dozen sentinels and pursued at least by as many more. Knowing that the pursuit would be maintained with the characteristic persistence of the Shawnees, he ran for several hundred yards at such a rate that he seemed to strain his system to its utmost tension. Then glancing furtively behind, and seeing nothing of his pursuers, he leaped against the trunk of a tree, and, with his rifle in his left hand, ascended with the agility of a monkey, and crouched panting and listening among the branches.

One—two—three—four—five dusky forms, a moment later, sped under him with the velocity of the wind, while all around their multitudinous tramp sounded like the passage of a drove of animals. Lindower listened till all was still, save the tumult in the village. Then, gliding down from his perch, he stole cautiously from tree to tree, till, judging himself at a safe distance, he continued his flight at his leisure.

The Spy, as we have seen, drew by far the greatest number after him. His danger was, consequently, greater than Lindower's. After running a considerable distance, he had recourse to the same stratagems, and with considerable success. Wheeling suddenly to the right, he escaped the greater part of the crowd, until the unexpected appearance of several warriors forced him back into what we have termed the main street again. Here he found himself followed by a swarm of men, women, boys and dogs, yelling, screaming, shouting and barking. Some of the Indian boys who came running from an opposite direction, and who seemed to understand the cause of the tumult, with a commendable bravery, threw themselves at full length on the ground so as to trip him as he ran. While in the act of springing lightly over one of these little fellows, the latter rose to his knees, when the Spy pitched headlong over him and was instantly buried out of sight by a living pile of bodies.

With an amount of strength almost superhuman, he arose to his feet, lifting these bodies with him, and seemed to bulge from them, like the sudden uprising of a volume of water from the ground. Swinging his rifle around, he sprung clear of the throng, and started off, leading the crowd again at his heels.

The reason of the Spy's eluding his pursuers thus far, was that only two or three men were among the dense mass that encompassed him. The chase seemed to be carried on like any other sport, the warriors quickly surrounding him so as to cut off his ultimate escape. In addition to this, the fugitive noticed that, while Lindower was repeatedly fired upon, not a shot had been discharged at himself. This was ample proof that his true character was at least suspected; consequently, his recapture unharmed was more desired than that of his friend.

All this time he was running, dodging, doubling and eluding his pursuers, as dextrously as when in the clearing. Once the brawny hand of a warrior was laid upon his shoulder, but as quick as lightning the Spy shot under his arm, overturning several who interposed in his way. It seemed impossible to retain any hold upon him, so skillful and eccentric were his movements. Now under their arms—now through their hands—now over their heads, in every imaginable direction, he kept up his flight, while his pursuers, taking knowledge from his different maneuvers, were gradually and more surely encompassing him.

In all these varied movements, it had been the aim of the Spy to gradually approach the edge of the wood, so that he could plunge into it at the last moment. But his turnings and twistings were so many that he had confused himself, and he saw to his surprise that he had made his way back to the very lodge from which he had fled. At this point, the chase assumed a ludicrous phase. The Spy had succeeded in placing his pursuers several yards behind him, and wheeling around the corner of the wigwam he dropped flat upon his face, and crawled in as close to the side as possible. This part being in shadow, the appearance of his body, hugging the ground and wall of the lodge as closely as possible, was the same as an ordinary pile of dirt, and, at any other time, would have been taken for such a natural deposit of the Indian lodge.

As the mass of the bodies swarmed into view, they poured on past without discovering their mistake, while an old squaw, panting and exhausted, halted, and staggering toward the lodge, seated herself directly on *the back of the Spy*. The 'atter, after so much exertion, could not restrain himself from breathing pretty deeply and rapidly, and his situation was certainly delicate and perilous. His first emotion was to laugh at his singular situation; his next thought was to quietly dispatch the squaw, and then rise and continue his flight; but, the squaw herself, probably frightened by the curious actions of the seat, gave a yell and sprung up. At the same instant the Spy threw his back up with great force, pitching her upon her head, and cutting off a most diabolical howl in its very utterance. He then sprung up and started off at the top of his speed, but had taken scarce a dozen steps, when he violently encountered an Indian. Looking up, he saw he was a helpless prisoner in the hands of Tecumseh.

## CHAPTER VI.

### TECUMSEH AND THE FOREST SPY.

*This was a strange chance.*
OTHELLO.

NOT a word passed between the Spy and Tecumseh. Both turned, as if by instinct, and walked toward the council-house, the crowd parting before them. There was no force used, for the prisoner, conscious that no effort of his could avail him, submitted with the best grace possible to his fortune. The council-house reached, the chief strode in, and motioned for the Spy to seat himself. This was done, when Tecumseh departed.

Several Indians remained in the house on guard, and the captive, yielding to his fatigue, fell into a feverish doze, which lasted till broad daylight. Then, recovering himself, and looking up, he saw he was in the presence of Tecumseh, Proctor, and several British officers. The room had been cleared of all others. The Spy instantly rose to his feet and stood before his captors, as if waiting for some demonstration from them. Proctor took upon himself the part of speaker. Stepping forward, he remarked, interrogatively:

"You were not pleased with your quarters last night, I presume?"

"I have been in better, and have been in worse."

"I have no doubt. And your companion—he seemed to entertain as poor an idea of Tecumseh's hospitality as did yourself."

"From what he said, I am led to believe it was not Tecumseh's hospitality he feared, so much as it was those of his own color and blood."

"Ah—yes, I understand. Perhaps he had good reason, too, especially when he makes such a visit as you did last night. But you come from General Harrison, I believe?"

"Yes, sir."

"Did he send any special message to me as well as to Tecumseh?"

"He and his soldiers intend bringing their message to you themselves, I b'lieve, in a few days."

"Do you know to whom you are speaking?" asked the Briton, threateningly."

"To General Proctor, commander of the British soldiers, I s'pose."

"Well, sir, time your answers accordingly, then, and remember, that your habitual recklessness will avail you nothing here."

Tecumseh made a sign to Proctor, when the latter asked:

"What brought you and Lin—your friend, I mean, here last night?"

"I stated my message then, I b'lieve."

"I am aware of what you said at that time—"

"Then what are you questioning me for?"

"I am aware, if you please, of what you gave as your message; but, I am as well aware that that was only a feint. Other motives brought you here. The *rescue of a friend*, perhaps? Was it not so?"

The Spy could not avoid a perceptible start at this unexpected question. Satisfied now that prevarication would avail him no longer, he deemed it not imprudent to give a truthful and straightforward answer.

"The rescue, or at least the hope of learning something about a captive, was the true cause of my coming here."

"A female captive, I believe?"

The Spy bowed without speaking.

"One taken a couple of years since, in the Creek country, and known as Laura Lindower, and whose brother, captured at the same time, and who subsequently escaped, paid us a short visit last night?"

The Spy bowed again.

"I suppose then," said Proctor, taking one of the Spy's locks between his fingers, "that you always dress your hair in this manner when making your calls?"

"As for that matter," returned the latter, without evincing the least embarrassment, "I believe a man in these days is at liberty to dress his hair to suit his own taste."

"And even if he choose to give his face a different hue, it is nobody's business."

"Nobody's business, General Proctor."

The imperturbable coolness with which these answers were given, served slightly to embarrass the General himself. He had calculated upon the prisoner evincing a confusion and perplexity when thus made aware that his identity was known; and, failing to see this, he was at a loss for a moment what to say further. Falling back a step or two, he commenced whispering to his officers, when Tecumseh himself stepped forward, with his haughty, majestic step, and in his full, deep and sonorous voice, asked:

"Why did my brother leave his lodge before the night had gone?"

"Because he believed it was his only chance if he had any idea of going at all."

"Are the children of your Great Father at Washington so plenty that he can send them thus into Tecumseh's camp?"

"I am not boasting, chief, when I say their number is like the leaves of your woods, and that, if you oppose them, they will sweep you from the earth."

As the Spy made this remark, he raised his eyes to Tecumseh's face. He saw the Indian's basilisk orbs fixed upon him, while the massive chest rose and sunk like a wave of the sea, with the thoughts that had been called to his mind. This agitation passed off in a moment, and he continued in his natural, deliberate tones:

"Are the children of your Father so numerous that he can lose his best men?"

"I've no doubt he cac'lates he must lose some of them afore he gets through, so he has made up his mind to *that*."

"He has scouts and runners that wander far from his camp."

"And, of course they know the risk they run as well as you or I."

"And he has *spies*," said the chief, in a whisper, deeper and more fearful than the muttering of thunder.

"That he has, chief, and no one knows the danger they run more than they do, themselves."

"What does my brother (General Harrison) do with the spies who come into *his* camp?"

"His ordinary custom is to shoot them; howsumever, he occasionally lets an *Injin* go, after he has scared them a little."

"My brother then *can* show mercy."

"A big lot of it; for, had he not been marciful in the years gone by, he would not have had these Injins to fight against. And when he takes a spy, if he is killed, he is decently shot, not roasted at the stake as are many of his own men by the Indians."

"Tecumseh does not burn his prisoners," said the chieftain, proudly.

The Spy knew that he had indeed been striving for years to abolish this horrid custom among his people, and he determined to profit by his knowledge of the fact.

"It is well known among my people that Tecumseh is merciful to his captives—far more merciful than are often his white allies, and it is believed he will ever treat them thus."

Tecumseh now gave way to the British commander, who approached and said in a more decided manner:

"You are the person known as the *Forest Spy*, are you not?"

"Such I am often called."

"What is your real name—your other?"

"That would do you no good to know, General Proctor. I am known among your people and among my own, only by the name that you have just spoken."

"Well, it makes little difference at any rate. The latter part of that name expresses your real character. That you can not deny?" The last sentence was half assertion, half question, given with the intention of sounding the prisoner.

"I deny nothing," he simply replied.

"You are aware, my friend, or rather enemy," continued Proctor, giving still more asperity to his tone, "what the penalty of the spy's degrading office is."

"Among nations professing to be human and civilized, it is a quick and speedy death, such as would have been the fate of that man by your side, had his character been known when he came among us."

"Very true. I am glad to see you do not try to shrink from the consequences your own rashness has invited. When you came to this Indian village did you expect to find his Majesty's representatives present?"

"I did not; otherwise I should have remained away."

"Exactly. Then your visit was to the Indians *alone*."

"So I have told you."

"Then to the Indians' mercies I consign you," said Proctor, turning his back and walking away.

The hapless prisoner was now left to himself for the space of half an hour. During that time Tecumseh stood with his arms folded and his eyes bent upon the ground, as if engaged in deep and serious thought. Proctor kept up a continued conversation with his officers in low, mumbling tones, varying it occasionally by glancing askance at the unfortunate American who had long since been doomed. As for the latter, he had folded his arms over the muzzle of his rifle, and resting his chin upon them, made the same picture that he might be supposed to present, when he had halted alone in the great wilderness to meditate upon some future course of action. He seemed entirely unconscious of the presence of any others, so rapt and absorbed was he.

Finally, the soldier, who has been mentioned as once acting as a spy, advanced to the prisoner and laid his hand upon his rifle.

"It can do you no good," said he, "and it will do you no harm if we take care of it for you. Your other weapons, if you please."

The captive looked up, and removing his arms from their resting-place, allowed the rifle to fall into the grasp of the soldier.

"Spitfire is a good piece," said the Spy, with some evidence of feeling, "and is a prize for any one who gets her. If she falls into *your* hands, I hope she'll do you as good service as she has the rightful owner. My knives, powder-horns and other trinkets are p'raps no better than others, and so you are welcome to them."

In a few moments, the captive was relieved of every thing in the way of arms, save such as nature had given him. At this Tecumseh looked up:

"My brother will go with me," he said, walking out of the lodge.

The Spy followed him through the devious windings of the village, for some time, and at length found that both were clear of the people and near the margin of the woods.

"I wish to talk with my brother. Will he strive to flee?"

"I give you my word, chief, that if you wish to converse with me, and will go where no other ears can hear us, I will make no attempt to run or get away."

Tecumseh unhesitatingly entered the woods, turning his back upon the Spy, who followed with his long, noiseless strides. Thus they walked for fully half a mile, penetrating deeper and deeper into the forest, until they had descended into a wild, desolate gorge. The chief then led the way for several rods through a dense thicket, and finally halted beneath a large, branching oak. The air was cold even to chilliness in this sequestered spot, and the place was so quiet that it indeed seemed "silent since the birth of time." At their feet flowed a small, rippling stream, through the velvety moss, as clear as the mountain air itself. While the summer sun was blazing in other places, in this spot an eternal twilight reigned. Not a breath moved the topmost branch of the gigantic oak, and the whirr of a bird, as it shot above their heads, was the only evidence that the region was ever visited by living creatures. Black and monstrous berries hung in clusters, rotting on their stems; huge limbs were moldering to pulp on the ground, while the deep-green grass was as soft and yielding as the sponge.

Tecumseh turned and spoke in a voice so low that it sounded like the rumbling from a cavern beneath them:

"Tecumseh knows the errand of the Forest Spy."

"So I suppose. It can not be gratified?"

"It may."

"Is she in the village?"

The chief inclined his head.

"May I see her before I die?"

He again signified assent.

"Has she been long in the village?"

"The White Lily has been in the lodges of the Shawnees for many moons."

"Is she the wife, the squaw of—of any of your people? Oh God! If she is I can not see her."

"The White Lily has been plucked by the hand of the red-man, but she has not fallen into his arms."

This, the Spy understood to mean that, while she had been taken from her home by the Indians, still she was not the squaw of any one. This knowledge was an infinite relief to him.

"And when, chieftain, may I see her?"

Tecumseh took a knife from his belt and handed it to the Spy. Then drawing another, he stepped back several paces and looked into his face. The white man met his gaze with a look as firm and defiant as his own. In this singular position the two remained for full ten minutes—looking into each other's eyes, reading each other's thoughts and determinations. The Spy understood the meaning of it all—knew the cause, saw the purpose, and was prepared for the issue. There was a story connected with those two opponents, strange in itself, but all-sufficient for this contest.

"I accept your challenge. If I fall?"

"You cross Tecumseh's path no more. You escape *death* by fire."

"If *you* fall?"

"My brother's feet are swift, and the path to his camp is clear. The prize he seeks shall be his."

"That is fair. Let us at work then!"

The hands of both closed upon their knife-handles. They surveyed each other with that fixed, piercing glance which is seen when two combating animals are brought for a moment face to face. The arm of the Shawnee chief was as rigid as a bar of iron, from the shoulder to the wrist. His left leg was about a foot in advance of the right, and bent somewhat more at the knee, and the muscles of each calf stood out like cords of steel. The left arm was bent in front of his chest as if to ward off an expected blow. The right hand was drawn back several inches, as if gathered to strike, and his whole posture was that of a thoroughly ferocious being about to leap upon a dangerous foe.

The attitude of the Spy was similar to the Shawnee's in many respects. His left leg was bent at the knee, but the right was perfectly straight to the foot, which was turned at right angles with its neighbor. His left arm crossed his breast in a diagonal direction, the hand resting against the right side of his belt. While the figure of the Indian was of one about to spring, that of the white man was of one prepared to receive the shock of a panther from some limb above him.

They stood thus a few seconds, when Tecumseh suddenly dropped his head, and flashed his keen knife above it with the rapidity of lightning. As if discharged by the same movement, the sharp report of a rifle resounded through the woods, and the weapon went spinning in splinters full twenty feet from his hand. Like a baffled lion he turned in his fury to see who had thus attempted his life. The Spy pointed with his knife to a clump of bushes on the edge of the gorge, from which a thin, bluish wreath of smoke was rising. Instantly, Tecumseh broke for the spot, followed by the white man, as intent as himself upon discovering the would-be assassin. The distance of his hiding-place and the nature of the ground were such that it required several minutes to reach it. When they did so, no trace was seen. Whoever he was he had made good his escape.

## CHAPTER VII.

### THE FAREWELL. A WONDERFUL OCCURRENCE.

> She stood a moment as a Pythoness
> Stands on her tripod, agonized and full
> Of inspiration gather'd from distress,
> When all the heart-strings, like wild-horses, pull
> The heart asunder; then, as more or less
> Their speed abated, or their strength grew dull,
> She sunk down on her seat by slow degrees,
> And bow'd her trembling head o'er throbbing knees.
> BYRON.

WHEN it was seen that the secret enemy had fled, Tecumseh signified to the Spy to follow him again to the village. The latter strongly hoped that he would take means to have the duel come off; but this hope was soon dispelled. After walking a few rods the chief halted, and taking his knife from his prisoner, pointed upward through the crevices of the tree-tops:

"When the sun is yonder, (pointing to a spot in the sky several degrees above the horizon,) the Spy of the Americans dies."

"And can I not see *her* before that time?"

"You shall remain with the White Lily until that time."

"That is all I ask. Tecumseh. Give me that privilege and I shall make no resistance to your designs, which God grant are nothing more than a merciful death. Another slight indulgence I would crave."

"What is it my brother wishes?"

A smile of shame crossed the features of the Spy as he replied:

"I would not go into her presence looking as I do now."

The chief pointed to a brook but a few yards away. Several minutes' ablution at this, sufficed to restore the countenance and hair of the captive to their natural appearance. At the edge of the woods they once more halted, and the Shawnee chief said:

"If my brother is left with the White Lily, will he run as he did last night?"

"Chieftain, I give you my word, that when on a parole of honor, I will make no attempt to escape. I will remain with her until you or your warriors come for me."

Tecumseh led the way through the village, his warriors, women and children respectfully giving way to his approach, and offering no rudeness to the prisoner. No one dared to oppose the imperial chieftain—the second Pontiac—or to question his actions. He moved among them like a despot, compelling reverence and obedience from every one.

The Indian village was laid out with considerable regularity, the streets winding and crossing each other in a much more convenient manner than in many of our own cities. The abundance of lodges of the same appearance changed the usually picturesque aspect of a collection of Indian wigwams to a monotonous tameness. After crossing and turning in numerous directions, Tecumseh, first motioning for his companion to remain outside, entered one of these lodges. In a few moments he emerged again, followed by several squaws, who separated, and took different paths.

"My warriors will call for the Spy," said the chief, making way for him to enter.

The Spy, with a beating heart and trembling step, pulled the fold of the wigwam aside, and entered, instinctively glancing about him, as he did so. He saw an ordinary Indian lodge, provided with the usual number of skins, cooking implements, etc. In the opposite corner, upon a rudely-fashioned seat, was —Laura Lindower—she for whom he had sought through two long years. She looked up as he entered and her expression of wonder changed to fear and consternation as she recognized her visitor. She trembled violently, and for a moment was unable to speak.

"I wonder not, Laura, at your fright in seeing me at this time and in this place," said the Spy, scarcely less agitated than herself.

She attempted to speak, and pointed to a seat.

"No, I have several hours to spend alone with you, and do not wish to sit down."

"Do you come alone—do you know any thing of my brother?"

"Gorman came with me, last night, but he has fled, and made good his escape from the knaves."

"Thank heaven! And yourself?"

"I have been arrested, Laura, as a spy, and this afternoon suffer death as a spy."

The manner of the captive had become more composed, and he spoke the words as he would have related any ordinary fact. The agitation of Laura Lindower, on the contrary, had become greater and greater, and, with the last announcement, she turned as pale as death. Springing to her feet, she approached the Spy; placing both hands in his, and saying, as she looked up in his face:

"And this because you sought me?"

"I brought a message from our General," he replied, closing his tremulous hands over those of his fair friend. He had never before, in all his long acquaintance with her, stood thus face to face, with his hands clasped upon hers. There was a novelty—a delight in this position which, despite his fearful surroundings, he experienced in all its fullness. The affection which had dwelt for years unexpressed in each heart, was now fully revealed in both their countenances. The visible presence of death at their side, brought them together, and swept away the restraint which had so long been an insuperable barrier to the Spy.

"If you came thus, how is it you are arrested as a spy, my friend?"

Laura Lindower trembled so violently that her "friend" led her back to her seat, placing himself beside her. Feeling somewhat the awkwardness of his own situation, he waited for her to recover composure, gazing mechanically at her dress, in the mean time. This was civilized, with the exception of the shawl or blanket—an Indian one—beautifully ornamented with beads and figures. Part of one foot was visible from beneath the folds of her dress, disclosing the instep of a beaded moccasin. The dress itself was a plain homespun, evidently brought from her distant home by the Indians at the time of her capture. The hair, of a light, silken color, was simply gathered at the back of the head, and was without ornament of any kind. Her features were well-proportioned, perhaps handsome. The face, naturally pale, gave an expression of mild beauty to the countenance—a fair index to the character of Laura Lindower. Some twenty-six or eight years of age, she had lived long enough to outgrow the impetuous feelings and impulsive passions of the young of her sex. She was a meek, subdued and affectionate woman—one whose affection, while mild and undemonstrative in itself, was as pure and lasting as that of the angels. Not the slightest advance had ever been made upon her part, during the years in which she had been acquainted with the Spy, and had received his visits. Interest grew into respect—friendship into affection. With one who could fully understand the peculiarities of the brave, simple-hearted lover, it could not well have been otherwise; and thus it came to pass, while their love for so many years had been an unspoken one, it was, nevertheless, deep, devoted, genuine.

The shock which Laura Lindower had received was so great, that with all her self-command it required considerable time to regain her wonted composure. With her face buried in her hands, until she felt able to meet the gaze of the noble man at her side, she looked up:

"Did Tecumseh grant you this interview?"

"He did. I asked it, and he told me I was to remain alone with you, until called away—to die."

"And is there no escape, my dear friend?"

"Not any, Laura; I can not make the attempt without breaking my word. But do not take it so hard like; I am sure," he added, with a wan smile, "that none ought to care more than I do about it, and I ain't afeard a bit."

While the Spy spoke, the yearning, soulful look of Laura was fixed steadfastly upon his face. Placing the palms of her hands on his shoulders, she said, in a changed and solemn voice:

"If you are so near death, my loved one, the moments are too precious to spend in unimportant conversation. I trust you are prepared to meet your God?"

This was the most trying moment of all to the Spy. With his knowledge of the religious feeling that ever actuated all of Laura Lindower's actions, he knew such a question would be made. She had, years before, when speaking of the great danger in which his life led him, hinted at his duty in being religiously prepared for it. On such occasions, it had been no difficult matter for him to escape with some promises and considerable self-recrimination; but the question was now too direct to admit of any but a direct reply. Dropping his gaze, and blushing like a child, he replied:

"As for the matter, Laura, it is hard to answer. I know I am not near as good, and never can be as good as you are, but—"

"Don't speak thus: it is not right. I pretend to no goodness, and you must think only of *yourself.*"

"I know—I know; but as I was saying, I can hardly answer you, Laura. Twice before, in my life, I have been in just such a scrape, when it seemed my race was about run. And that is many years ago, when I was much younger and rasher than I am now. I made a great noise about being served so bad, and all that, and both times the matter ended by my getting clear after all."

"But you do not answer my question," gently chided his listener.

"I answer, then, in this way," replied the Spy, looking over her face at the side and top of the lodge, as if searching for words: "*I* do not feel afeard. I've fetched up so often with death, that I've been willing to go under at any time. I never have done much praying, like you have, and when I come to stand afore the Good Being above, I expect I can say little in my own favor. I can tell him, howsomever, that I've never struck a redskin, 'cept when I thought it had to be done, and I think when General Harrison comes along to heaven, he'll say a good word to the Lord for me, as will a great many of the other Generals we've had. And General Harrison's recommendation is something I am always proud of, and is something that I feel sure will do me a good turn, when our accounts are wound up."

The perfect simplicity and seriousness with which this was uttered almost forced a smile to the face of his fair questioner; but she added, in an impressive tone:

"Other persons' words and recommendations can do you no good in that awful hour. Every one must render his own account. I know you have done many noble deeds in your life, but these will avail you nothing, unless you are prepared to meet God. Do not waste words, my dearest friend; do you not *know* that you are unprepared?"

"Yes," replied the Spy, in a tone full of self-abasement and emotion.

"You have to make preparation. Let us not wait. I will first pray for you. Come, we will kneel down at this moment."

She sunk devoutly upon her knees, and when the trembling Spy had done the same, her voice arose in supplication. Its tones were low, but so earnest, so full of tender interest and love, that every word went like a dagger to his heart. Never before had he felt his soul's guiltiness as at that moment, and, ere she had finished, he followed her pleadings with his own tremulous petition for grace in God's eyes.

They remained a long time upon their knees. It was an impressive sight—this weak woman guiding the famous *Forest Spy*, whose wonderful deeds were known far and wide, to the throne of grace. When they arose, he instantly remarked that he felt a much better man—so much like dying right away!

"I am so glad you feel so! I knew you would. When you are led forth to die, think not of escape, though I would gladly have you free if that were possible. But, continue praying—pray for your tormentors—spend your last moments in prayer, and I will do nothing else for you as long as you live. God is good; and oh! my dearest friend, He will not desert you in your last moments. Do you know *how* you are to suffer death?"

"I am not certain; it rests with Tecumseh."

"Tecumseh is merciful. He has done all in his power to abolish the practice of burning prisoners, among his different tribes, and I do not think he would allow his worst enemy to suffer torture."

The Spy made no reply to this remark, and both remained silent for a considerable time. The expression upon each face was solemn, yet resigned. They seemed to have fallen in precisely the same reverie—melancholy in itself, yet not without its sweetness. The minutes thus flew unnoted, and Laura was only made sensible of the lapse of time when the curtain-door was pulled aside, and an Indian signaled for the Spy to come forth. Laura sprung up in dismay, to ask in the Shawnee tongue, if the hour had arrived. Being answered in the affirmative, she requested him to beseech Tecumseh to grant a respite of a few moments. As the warrior disappeared, she turned toward the Spy, who said:

"Why do you wish to postpone the hour? I have been praying to God for the last two or three hours, and am ready to go this minute."

The face of Laura Lindower was irradiated by a heavenly expression when she heard these cheering words. Her mild blue eyes were luminous with a holy light as she answered:

"We will pray together once more; but, how did you know I made the request?"

"The Shawnee tongue is as well known to me as the English, and so are a dozen other of their lingoes; but your messenger has been quick—there he is!"

Laura turned and approached the opening. The Indian told her that Tecumseh had complied with her request, but that the prisoner would be led forth at the expiration of the time mentioned. She again walked toward the Spy, who arose, joined one of his hands with hers, and the two knelt down.

Together they prayed, long and earnestly—in low, solemn tones. The united petitions, ascended to the Great Throne together and were answered.

When they arose the face of the messenger was visible.

The Spy placed his arm around the neck of Laura, looking down in her radiant, upturned countenance.

"And now, Laura, we separate. I don't know what is in store for you; but whatever it is, I know I shall see you in the Good Place above, changed to one of those angels. You know my name, where I came from, and why I have kept up my disguise so long. Before coming here, I prepared a small package, containing several letters addressed to different people, who are old friends, and who've known nothing of me for years. Here's the package. If you are ever given the chance, give them to the ones that they are directed to. Don't take this matter to heart. Remember, I don't care for it. Good-by—good-by."

The tears were blinding his eyes. Stooping he hastily kissed the cheek of his loved one—the first time in his life. He tried to say something more, but the words choked him, and removing his arm, he moved toward the door. Laura held his hand and walked with him. As he was stepping out, she grasped him with extraordinary power, and attempted to speak. He brushed the tears from his eyes and looked at her. Twice she essayed to utter her farewell, but was unable; and feeling his own strength giving way, and hardly conscious of what he did, he turned and passed out of the lodge.

When Laura Lindower saw that she was alone, she sunk upon the ground and remained as one dead, for several hours.

As the Forest Spy passed into the open air, his usual self-possession returned. He looked around with an undaunted front for his enemies. To his surprise, four warriors only were present. Some great and exciting circumstance seemed to have absorbed the attention of others. Nothing was to be seen of Tecumseh or the British officers—something extraordinary had certainly happened to the village.

The first act of his guards was to bind his arms behind him. This was done most effectually, by passing thongs around them at the elbows and wrists, and drawing them firmly together.

So powerfully was the tension, and so unnatural their position, that not a pound of their strength was available. They now were of no more use than if they had been severed from his body. Each of the Indians was covered with war-paint—the black stains on their faces being crossed with crimson lines, giving them the appearance of gashes, and rendering their disguise complete. A large, muscular, half-naked fellow was the leader. He simply directed their movements without taking part in them himself. Each carried two knives and a tomahawk, and were unremitting in their watch over the prisoner.

Passing by the side of the lodge—an Indian walking on either side, one behind him, and the leader in front—they soon made their way to the boundary of the village. Here they halted a moment, and the leading savage looked back, as if in expectation of some signal. Receiving this, they moved on again into the woods.

Tramp, tramp, tramp, passed the silent and grim executioners, deeper and deeper into the forest. The observant eyes of the Spy soon showed him that they were following the same course that he and Tecumseh had taken a few hours before. As he reached the spot where the chieftain had revealed his face to him, he could not forbear looking over his shoulder at the sun. It was in that part of the heavens which, he had been given to understand, would announce the hour of his death.

Onward they tramped, down through the dark, desolate gorge, across the thicket, up to the trunk of the oak where he had stood with Tecumseh. A glance sufficed to show the Spy the meaning of these singular movements. Around the foot of the oak was arranged a circle of fagots, while a larger pile lay some ten or twelve feet behind. The prisoner, although he had received hints of death by fire, did not believe that he had been doomed to suffer at the stake. He had full confidence in the merciful reputation of the great Shawnee chief, and did not believe he would dare, in the face of this, to inflict such an outrage upon a person as well known as himself. But, he saw now that he had been deceived. Indulging his malignant enmity of the white man, Tecumseh had sentenced him to the stake and appointed four of his warriors to do it in secret, while he himself remained away, and took no part in the barbarity.

As the Spy saw these fearful preparations, a wild resolve to escape seized him, and he looked about him to see his chances. But this sudden gleam of hope was extinguished immediately. The Indians were fully prepared for any such hopeless attempt.

"I submit," said the Spy, "I can do nothing. My last hour has finally come, and I've lived long enough to go through this torture without wincing. God sustain me, and receive my soul at last."

He was perfectly passive in their arms, as they led him to the tree. Another thong was now doubled, passed through his elbows, and knotted upon the opposite side of the tree. His feet were next bound together and fastened to the trunk in the same fashion. A third ligature crossed his breast, and being drawn very tight around the tree, compressed his arms in a most painful manner. Still a fourth bond held his knees together, and made his position as immovable as that of the oak itself.

While two Indians had been busily engaged in thus securing their captive, the leader, standing back a few paces, had directed the third to place the fagots in position. All three now engaged themselves at this, and in a few moments it was piled above his knees, so close that the flames must lick his face. The leader cut numerous green twigs with his tomahawk, threw them upon the pile, and loosened the others so as to give the blaze plenty room for play.

All these movements the Spy had watched with a wandering, mechanical gaze, but with thoughts fixed only upon his rapidly approaching dissolution. He was constantly praying, and remembering the injunction of Laura Lindower, he even supplicated for his tormentors. His mind was absent, and, for the time, he was insensible of his surroundings. He was suddenly called to a sense of his situation by a puff of smoke rising in his face. Looking downward, he saw an Indian bent, and in the act of firing the fagots. Two or three twigs had caught, and a fork of flame was twisting through the crevices in the kindlings. A small column of tremulous smoke, ascending directly in his face, already made him cough for breath.

The Indian now arose and moved away, and in grim silence the four awaited the progress of the flames. The fire burned rapidly for a few minutes, then the fagots fell together and it was extinguished. The wood was full of sap, and required careful kindling before it would burn. The savage who had taken upon himself the office of executioner, stepped forward and carefully rearranged the fagots and kindlings. In a moment they were again fired, and again the flame commenced ascending. A second time the framework of green twigs tumbled together and extinguished the blaze completely. The attempt was made a third time, with no better result.

It was now plain that the fire needed more dry stuff for kindling ere it would communicate with the entire mass. The leader, in an angry voice, commanded the three to seek it at once, and all moved forward to do so. These three started simultaneously, and moved together past the tree, to some bushes about a dozen yards behind it. (The reader is now desired to notice particularly the movements of all four.) Here they commenced breaking and cutting twigs, but, finding little of the required dryness, they necessarily made but tedious progress. After admonishing them, several times, to use more haste, the leader strode forward, in an angry mood, to assist and hurry them. He broke off numerous branches from the trees, and soon had collected quite a quantity. Speaking to the others, each of the four moved back again toward the tree, carrying a bundle of the "kindlings" in his arms. They reached the tree, passed round it, then threw down their loads. Then ascended such a yell as only the demons of the lower world can be supposed to give. All drew back in blank amazement:—*their prisoner, the Forest Spy, was gone!* The fagots had been scattered around as if they had been kicked thus by his feet; but, not a sign of a thong or ligature was to be seen. Raising his hand to enforce silence, the leader, in a low and threatening tone, directed his men to examine the ground. The three did so, again and again, and so minutely that the track of a fawn would not have escaped their eyes; but they discovered nothing, save their own footmarks. *No one besides themselves and the prisoner had entered this spot!* Neither had any one left it! Most unaccountable and strange was the occurrence.

When the three warriors made known the results of their search, the leader answered in an impressive voice:

"'Tis Wahcondah," and moved away, they following after him. Passing through the gorge they encountered Tecumseh, who was raging like a tiger. He had heard their yell of disappointment, and was hastening to ascertain its meaning. A few words explained all.

"The tree! the tree! search the tree!" he exclaimed, dashing toward it. The others followed, and, in a moment, all stood beneath it. Tecumseh immediately sprung up in the limbs and was instantly followed by the leader of the others. A thorough search—one that discovered every bird's nest in it—was made among the branches, but with no success. The trunk was also examined and found to be perfectly sound. As they were descending, an exclamation from one of those on the ground drew their attention. The savage, on the very spot where the four had been collecting their brush, picked up the thongs with which the prisoner had been bound. They were cut and torn in shreds, and several were stained with blood. Upon discovering this, the Indian instantly dropped the pieces as if they had been so many poisonous vipers. Tecumseh approached and looked at them. The leader did the same without saying a word.

A minute later, Tecumseh, with a troubled and moody brow, moved slowly back through the gorge toward the village. Behind him came his four warriors, equally silent and gloomy.

## CHAPTER VIII.

### THE BEGINNING OF THE END.

The time of universal peace is near:
Prove this a prosperous day, the three-nook'd world
Shall bear the olive freely.
ANTONY AND CLEOPATRA.

Lest our readers may suspect us guilty of trifling with their credulity, we hasten to explain an occurrence that probably seems as mysterious to them as it did to Tecumseh and his warriors. The Spy, it will be recollected, was most securely bound to the tree, and in so hopeless a position that he had given over all hope and was occupying himself solely with preparing for his dissolution, which seemed so fearfully near. The reader will further remember that one of the four executioners acted the part of leader. When we reveal the identity of this Indian, half the mystery will be explained. He was no other than Nockwynee, the Creek, who had been befriended by the Spy, when discovered in the house of Gorman Lindowen, on the night in which our story opened. He was a chief of his nation—bold, revengeful and bloodthirsty—one who never forgave an injury nor forgot a kindness. These traits had won for him a place high in the confidence of Tecumseh, who intrusted many cherished schemes to his execution. Nockwynee knew of the Spy's visit and of his danger from Tecumseh. When his identity became known, and he had been recaptured, the Shawnee chieftain proposed to Nockwynee to burn him. He readily promised to do it, and the spot which we have described was the one chosen. Nockwynee selected three Shawnees, and painting himself so that he could not be recognized by the Spy, made his preparations—fully determined to save his benefactor if it cost him his own life.

The green fagots were purposely gathered by him, the kindlings were intentionally so slight that they could accomplish nothing. The Creek had arranged the whole scheme, and carried it out most admirably. The instant the three Shawnees passed behind and away from the oak in search of the dry fuel, a low whistle attracted the attention of the Spy. Looking up he saw the black orbs of the leader fixed upon him with a curious expression. Before he could satisfy himself of what this meant, the Creek drew his knife, and whispered: "Me Nockwynee!" Immediately after he called out in an angry tone to the savages, bidding them to be more expeditious, starting toward them. In doing this, he passed on the left of the tree, and halted for a second by the Spy. The Indians' backs were turned toward him, and, of course, they suspected nothing. With his eyes fixed upon their movements, and with the Spy himself in the field of vision, he drew his keen knife, with the quickness of lightning, across the thongs at the elbows, wrists and waist. Then, without looking at the Spy, he handed him his knife and passed on, still urging the Indians to hasten their preparations.

The Spy himself was now free with the exception of his feet. These were instantly liberated, and he was left to his unfailing resources to complete an escape the most remarkable of all that had occurred to him in a long and eventful life. In that dreadful moment, he did not forget the great risk which Nockwynee ran for him. He knew the Creek would never survive the discovery of treachery upon his part. Accordingly he gathered all the thongs in his left hand, forced his knife down in his belt and, springing nimbly upward, caught a limb and ascended the tree in a twinkling. He had just time to ensconce himself in the thick foliage, when his escape was discovered. We have pictured the feigned consternation of Nockwynee, and the genuine horror of the others. Scarce thirty feet from them sat the object that had caused all this, peering down through the leaves, and shaking as if he had the ague with his suppressed laughter. He saw Nockwynee cast more than one stealthy glance upward as though he did not feel perfectly at ease, and he witnessed, with the most genuine gusto, the manner in which the superstition of the others was wrought upon.

When they had turned and were at a safe distance, he passed out on one of the limbs, threw the thongs to the ground, (after cutting them in many pieces, and staining them with the blood from a wound made by his own hurried efforts to free his feet,) sprung to the close limb of a heavy sycamore, passed to its opposite side, and, dropping lightly to the earth, made creditable use of his legs. He came within a hair's breadth of meeting Tecumseh—hearing his heavy, mad tramp just in time to hide until the furious man had passed. He could hardly restrain himself from rushing upon the doubly savage foe, when he reflected what a fate had been planned by him. Regard for Nockwynee prevented this act. When the chief descended into the gorge, the Spy resumed his flight at a rate which would have made pursuit sheer folly. He felt a great desire to acquaint Laura with his glorious fortune, and he once paused, half determined to risk a run through the village for this purpose; but knowing that she must soon hear of it, he kept on, thanking Heaven again and again for this most miraculous adventure of his life.

When Laura Lindower recovered from the stupefied state into which she had fallen, the two squaws who generally occupied the lodge with her were present, regarding her with looks of wonder and inquiry. Recalling what had occurred, it was only by the most painful effort that she maintained her self-control. While still trying to calm her agitation, she heard a great clamor upon the outside. Women and children were running to and fro, uttering exclamations, the meaning of which for a time she could not understand. Suddenly a small Indian boy burst into the wigwam, and revealed the startling fact that Forest Spy had escaped—that he had been carried away by the Manitou of the white people.

It would prove in vain to picture Laura Lindower's feeling at this intelligence. For a time she could not realize that it could be true; but when all doubt was removed, and the minutest particulars were made known, she sunk upon her knees, and in the presence of several squaws and warriors, returned thanks to Providence.

The escape, as related to her, seemed unaccountable. So

marvelous indeed did it appear, that she could only explain it upon supernatural grounds, and regard it as a direct interference of Heaven. When she learned, however, a few hours later, that Nockwynee was the principal one of the appointed executioners, a suspicion of the truth flashed across her mind. She remembered seeing this Indian upon the night their house was attacked, and she recalled the mention afterward made of him by the Spy. Further than this, Nockwynee himself had given her to understand that he was sorry for this act of his, and would do what he could to set her at liberty again. With her knowledge of Indian character she believed him a true friend and placed great confidence in him. So wily and acute was this Creek, that, although Tecumseh's deadliest enemy, his disaffection was suspected by none.

Leaving these matters, however, for the present, we must turn to more important events that are already beginning to move. Although the scenes of this narrative are laid in the war of 1812, we have scarcely referred to the principal occurrences of public interest, presuming the reader to be sufficiently well acquainted with their history; but, as our drama, from this point, hinges, in a great measure, upon the closing events of the war in the North-west, we subjoin a brief summary of the deeds in that quarter, up to the present point.

After the fruitless siege of Fort Meigs, in the spring of 1813, by Proctor and Tecumseh, the Canadian militia were disbanded, and the different Indians stationed at separate cantonments. The Miamis and Wyandots were sent up the Detroit river to Maguagua; the Pottawatomies up Rouge river, and the Chippewas were permitted to return home. Proctor employed these different parties as scouts and spies, and was regularly informed of the condition and movements of the American forces. Deeming the occasion a suitable one, General Proctor attacked Fort Meigs for the second time, in the latter part of July. At this assault, Tecumseh headed eight hundred Indians, and by the execution of an ingenious stratagem, came within a hair's breadth of carrying the fort. Finding, however, by the coolness of General Clay, the British troops sailed around into Sandusky bay, for the purpose of attacking Fort Stephenson, at Lower Sandusky (now Fremont), Ohio. A portion of the Indians proceeded across by land, while Tecumseh, at the head of two thousand warriors, took up a position in the Black Swamp, between Fort Meigs and Sandusky, for the purpose of cutting off any reinforcements, or to fall upon the camp at Seneca, as might be deemed best.

The memorable defense of Fort Stephenson, by Captain Croghan, effectually ended the offensive operations of Proctor and Tecumseh in this quarter, and transferred the operations to another section. Proctor returned by water to Malden, with his troops; while Tecumseh and his warriors passed around the head of Lake Erie, to join him at that place. During the stay at the head of the lake, the incidents recorded in the preceding chapters took place.

A few days later the Forest Spy and Gorman Lindower were retraversing the western shore of Lake Erie in the vicinity of the now deserted Indian camp. The sagacity of the former had brought them together, when they exchanged experiences and held a consultation. Knowing that the sudden movement of Indians in crossing the Detroit had reference to some important combination, they determined to follow after them, and, as soon as their intentions were discovered, to report them to General Harrison. They were about a mile from the lake, traversing a broad belt of forest. Feeling secure from danger, they were whiling away the hours in pleasant chat, the major part, of course, being done by the Spy.

"I'm thinking," he remarked, after a moment's silence, "that the villains, with that bloody Proctor, will fetch up on t'other side the lake, and give the Gineral battle. What's your idee?"

"S'pose so."

"And it'll be a mighty big scrimmage too, fur it's purty sartain it'll decide matters in these parts. If Proctor wasn't such a coward, I'd have a great deal of fear for our boys; but, that British Gineral is no more fit to lead soldiers than you are, Gorman, which means nothing ag'in your courage, but that if you should say, 'Charge!' or 'Fire!' it would be the last of you, because it would be more words than you ever dare to speak out at one time."

"Umph!"

"Decided fact, Gorman, which isn't, consequently, to your discredit. Howsumever, as I's saying, there's a desperate scrimmage only a few days ahead. I must take part in that! Tecumseh has been wanting to settle accounts with me for a long time, and—"

"What accounts?"

"You've had plenty chances to know, Gorman, if you'd only kept your eyes about you; but it seems you're resolved that I shan't have the time to say a word, the way you're interrupting me. As I was saying when you put me out, Tecumseh and I have a long account to square up, and I'm as anxious to do it as he is. I shall try and make my arrangements, so that we shall meet face to face in the coming battle."

"What battle? Umph!"

"It seems, Gorman, besides being talkative this morning,

your ideas are rather scanty—seem to have left you for the present, as it were. Since that affair at Fort Stephenson, it's plain Proctor is scar't more'n ever, and is retreating up toward Canada, while our own Gineral—bless his soul! I hope he'll be President some day—while our own Gineral, as I said, when you was getting rea'ly to interrupt me ag'in, is follering on after them, as fast as the legs of his soldiers can carry them."

"How'd you know that, say!"

"It's the natur' of the animal, and I'm as sartain of it as I am that we're walking together this minute. We're between two fires, as it were."

"Umph!"

"The tongue, the Good Book says, is an unruly member, and it's your bounden duty, Gorman, to put a curb upon yours. Your habit of making promiscuous remarks may get you into trouble some day—Oh! you needn't look so surprised and innocent. Advice is meant for your good, and you should take it so."

"Thunder and blazes! who's talking now, I sh'd like to know!"

"Yourself, Gorman, yourself, and talking rather louder than I'd advise people to do in these parts. Like as not some of Tecumseh's men may still be hangin' around here, and, overhearing your words, report them at head-quarters. It would make it bad for you."

"Umph!!" angrily exclaimed Lindower, walking ahead faster than ever.

"Softly, Gorman, softly; you're getting rash ag'in. You may—"

"Hark!" exclaimed Lindower, suddenly halting.

A loud explosion like the booming of thunder reverberated through the woods, and was heard for several seconds, dying away in sullen echoes in the distance. The two hunters stood as motionless as statues, until perfect silence again reigned, when Lindower asked in a whisper:

"Was that thunder?"

"The sky is clear and free of clouds, but such things do happen sometimes. When I was scouting once for Mad Anthony—"

"There it is again!"

Two reports, almost simultaneous, were now heard. The breeze blowing in from the lake, they resembled the bursting of thunderbolts, but a few hundred yards distant. All three peals had come from precisely the same point.

"It's from the lake," exclaimed the Spy, "and it's the thunder of cannon!"

As he spoke, he strode away through the woods in the direction of Lake Erie, followed by his companion, who, curiously enough, was not half so excited as himself. As they pressed on, the reports came faster and faster, and when they dashed down upon the shore of the lake, the booming was incessant. Several miles out they saw a great bank of smoke slowly spreading outward and upward in vast, rolling volumes, amid which the flashes of artillery were seen like lightning flaming through the clouds. Within this, like a forest stripped of its vegetation, were visible the masts and yards of vessels gradually centering toward each other. From this network of rigging, streamed the blood-red cross of King George, and the Star-Spangled Banner of the United States, passing and mingling with each other, seemingly in inextricable confusion. Too far removed to engage in this splendid naval battle were visible the vessels of both nations, hastening toward the exciting scene. The huge sails bellying outward with the strong breeze, the black hulls through whose port-holes the shotted cannon were gaping, the decks crowded with eager men, the water curling and foaming from their prows—all formed a sublime and thrilling sight. As the vessels came nigh enough, they rounded to, and delivered their tremendous broadsides, the smoke of which was wafted in a cloud through their own rigging. They then hurried on, and soon disappeared in the vast field of vapor. Now and then, a breeze swept away a portion of this, and the great, dark hulls were seen belching flame and death, and the masts and rigging crashing to the decks. At first, the fire of the enemy was directed principally against the flag-ship "Lawrence," which underwent a most murderous and dreadful fire.

From their position the Spy and Lindower saw the gallant commander leave her in an open boat when she was in a sinking condition, and carry his flag to the "Niagara," running a terrible gauntlet before the feat was accomplished. The brilliant exploit of the "Niagara," in running the enemy's line, and pouring successive broadsides in upon five of their vessels at half pistol-shot distance, was also witnessed.

The battle of Lake Erie has been too often described for us to reproduce its particulars here. Suffice it to say that, at four o'clock in the afternoon, the remainder of the American squadron came up, and the surrender of Commodore Barclay was made. When this was observed, the excitable feelings of the Spy once more got the better of him, and swinging his hat over his head, he cheered again and again. Dissatisfied with this, he ran down the beach to the edge of the water, and danced and yelled like an insane Indian. Lindower himself seemed unmoved, though more than once his fine gray eye kindled with the enthusiasm of his comrade, but he did not even stir from his position, much less join in the mad pleasure.

"Gorman," said the Spy, "that's been one of the greatest battles ever fought in this country, and one of the biggest kind of vict'ries. If I only had Spitfire here, which I'm afeared I'll never see ag'in, I believe I would have drawed bead on some of them Britishers. Howsumever, as I's saying, you must guard ag'in excitement. You ought to l'arn to look on such a fight as that—"

"Now, hold on," said Lindower, wheeling upon his companion; "I won't stand any more of that, I'll be derned if I will."

The Spy indulged in a clear, ringing laugh, and patting him good-naturedly upon his shoulder, said:

"We've known each other long enough, Gorman, to understand each other; but, it's getting well on toward night, and, as Tecumseh and Proctor are somewhere in these parts, it's time we were on the move."

With this, the two moved forward, shaping their course with the western extremity of the lake. At night they encamped within the woods, and at early light resumed their journey. When opposite Malden, the Spy's keen eye sought and soon found an Indian canoe. In this, they embarked at nightfall and crossed to the Canada shore. Here they found the combined force of the British and Indians preparing for a retreat further into Canada. With such a large army this necessarily occupied a considerable period, and our two friends remained reconnoitering in the vicinity for several days, during which time the ready penetration of the Forest Spy discovered unmistakable signs of disaffection among the Indian allies. The defeat of the British squadron lessened respect for their power, while the vacillation of Proctor disgusted Tecumseh. It is well known that the latter told the British General to his face to return to his *mother*, who would take care of him.

Toward the middle of September, as the preparations were completed for commencing the retreat, the Spy noticed a gathering of the Indians and British and suspected that the former had demanded a council. Approaching as nigh as was prudent, he ascended a tree to watch the proceedings. He saw Tecumseh rise to speak, and his rich, sonorous tones made every word distinctly audible. The intervening space over which the sound passed, made his emphasized words follow his gestures, and gave a peculiar force to his language, which was directed to Proctor himself, who seemed equally interested in, and displeased with, the speech.

"Father, listen to your children! You now have them all before you.

"The war before this, our British father gave the hatchet to his red children, when our old chiefs were alive. They are now dead. In that war our father was thrown on his back by the Americans; and our father took them by the hand without our knowledge; and we are afraid our father will do so again this time.

"Summer before last, when I came forward with my red brethren, and was ready to take up the hatchet in favor of our British father, we were told not to be in a hurry, that he had not yet determined to fight the Americans.

"Listen! when war was declared, our father stood up and gave us the tomahawk, and told us that he was then ready to strike the Americans; that he wanted our assistance, that he would certainly get our lands back, which the Americans had taken from us.

"Listen! you told us that time to bring forward our families to this place and we did so; and you promised to take care of them, and they should want for nothing, while the men would go and fight the enemy; that we need not trouble ourselves about the enemy's garrisons; that we knew nothing about them, and that our father would attend to that part of the business. You also told your red children that you would take good care of your garrison here, which made our hearts glad!

"Listen! when we were last at the Rapids, it is true we gave you little assistance. It is hard to fight people who live like ground-hogs.

"Father, listen! our fleet has gone out; we know they have fought; we have heard the great guns; but we know nothing of what has happened to our father with one arm.* Our ships have gone one way, and we are much astonished to see our father tying up every thing and preparing to run away the other without letting his red children know what his intentions are. You always told us to remain and take care of our lands. It made our hearts glad to hear that was your wish. Our great father, the king, is head and you represent him. You always told us you would never draw your foot off British ground; but now, father, we see that you are drawing back, and we are sorry to see our father doing so without observing the enemy. Our father is like a fat dog, that carries his tail on his back, but when affrighted, drops it between his legs and runs off.

"Father, listen! the Americans have not yet defeated us by land; neither are we sure that they have done so by water; we, therefore, wish to remain here and fight our enemy, should they make their appearance. If they defeat us, we will then retreat with our father.

"Father, you have got the arms and ammunitions which our great father sent for his red children. If you have an idea of going away, give them to us, and you may go and welcome, for

* The Commodore of the British squadron had but one arm.

us. Our lives are in the hands of the Great Spirit. We are determined to defend our lands, and if it be His will, we wish to leave our bones upon them."*

General Proctor made a short reply to this, but his voice was not loud enough to make his words audible, and, sliding down from his perch, the Spy returned to his companion.

"There's trouble in the camp," said he, "and I hope it'll break out in something or other, right away."

"Umph!" replied his companion.

"Tecumseh is mad at Proctor, and I believe has half made up his mind to leave him."

"Hope he will."

"So do I. To-night will tell. I must keep a close watch of affairs, and like enough when we return to the Gineral we'll have considerable information for him."

It was but a few hours after the delivery of this speech, that the Spy detected a movement among the Indians. A large number passed down to the shore, and, embarking in their canoes, crossed the strait to the American side, but Tecumseh was not among them. The Spy noticed him passing to and fro, and saw that he was undecided what course to pursue.

"I pray heaven you may go, too, Tecumseh," muttered the Spy. "The Gineral would then make short work of them Britishers. However much I'd like to meet you and settle that affair, I'm willing to put it off for the benefit of others. Ah! me, but I'm much afeard them Sioux and Chippewas won't let you go."

Such, indeed, was the case. Tecumseh was so enraged at the repeated deceptions of Proctor, that he had half determined to draw off his followers from his army. The Shawnees would have willingly done this, as they shared the same feeling as their chief; but the Sioux and Chippewas declared that they could not withdraw, and at the same time affirmed as positively that they would have no leader but Tecumseh himself.

"The battle-field has no terrors for me," replied the chieftain. "I have no fear of death, and if you insist upon my remaining, I shall do so."

From the actions of the Indians Forest Spy saw with pain that the greater part of them had concluded to remain and take part in the coming battle. The same day the savages removed their children to a place opposite the river Rouge. This was proof sufficient, and he watched their further movements with the greatest interest.

That evening, Gorman Lindower proposed that they should

* This speech was actually delivered by Tecumseh on the occasion mentioned.

now ven'ure into the Indian camp, believing that the rescue of his sister could be effected. The Spy at first was disposed to adopt the suggestion, but, after a few minutes' reflection, decided against it. Every thing indicated that they were upon the eve of a great battle, and a heavy responsibility was upon their shoulders. They already possessed information which was valuable to the American forces, and to engage in a *private* enterprise at this time, would hamper their movements too much. Besides, the Spy had reasons of his own for believing that the escape of his loved one could be effected more certainly immediately after the battle than before it.

The next day the retreat of the Indians was continued toward the Thames. The Spy and Lindower still followed, watching every movement with a jealous eye, and sometimes exposing themselves to a most fearful peril in their efforts to gain more certain information. On the second of October, the combined forces reached "Dalson's Farm," where they encamped. The Spy at this time was within a mile of the encampment, and was following the main road, it being his intention to approach as closely as possible, that evening, and after learning all that he could, to hasten to Harrison with it. Lindower was a couple of miles further behind him, waiting for his return at an appointed rendezvous. The Spy was walking cautiously, when he saw, about half a mile ahead, a horse and carriage descending a hill and coming on a brisk trot toward him. Concluding it best to be seen by no one at such a time, he stepped aside from the road and waited for the carriage to pass. Soon he heard the tramp of the horse's feet and the rattle of wheels. He peered out, and, to his surprise saw Proctor and Tecumseh seated together in a top-gig, talking in a very earnest but friendly manner.

"There's something to learn," muttered the Spy, springing out and running behind the gig, much after the manner of a boy when "catching behind." He even laid his hands on the awkward, rocker-like springs and jogged merrily forward, smiling at his own appearance, and listening to the words of those in front. The top being up, he was thoroughly protected from discovery. The gig was a rickety affair, and the spokes rattled so much that he could only get the drift of their conversation. He found it to be principally in regard to selecting a battle-ground.

The brisk trot of the horse was kept up until they reached a deep, unfordable stream which flowed into the Thames at a place called Chatham. Here the animal was reined down to a walk, and the words of the two leaders were distinctly heard. They rode all around the spot, the audacious Spy still striding behind, so pleased with the information he was obtaining that he helped push the vehicle up the swells and held it back in descending them.

The battle-ground seemed to please greatly both Tecumseh and Proctor. They examined it carefully and the latter remarked, as they were about to return:

"Here we will either defeat General Harrison, or lay our bones."

"It is a good place," returned the chief, "and when I look at these two streams, they will remind me of the Wabash and the Tippecanoe."

"That is decided then, and we will now return to camp; we may be running some risk in leaving the guard so far behind."

The horse started off on a trot so suddenly that the Spy was nearly jerked off his feet. The last words of Proctor made him look out from behind the gig, and ranging his sight along the side of the animal, he saw, but a short distance away, some eight or ten armed Indians, the body-guard of the two leaders, awaiting their return. Singular as it may seem, they were but several hundred yards from the Spy when he sprung out from the road-side, and yet not one observed him. He was noticed shortly after, trotting behind the gig, but every one supposed him one of Proctor's scouts; and thus, unknown to himself at the time, he ran a double risk.

"I guess I'll leave just now," he muttered, letting go the springs and whisking off to one side. "I've learned plenty, and now I'll make my call on the Gineral, for he must be wondering what has become of me and Gorman."

## CHAPTER IX.

### THE BATTLE OF THE THAMES.

> The shout
> Of battle now began, and rushing sound
> Of onset.   .   .   .   .   .
> 'Twixt host and host but narrow space was left.
> MILTON.

THE Forest Spy hastened to the rendezvous, where he found Lundower, and they both commenced their return toward Malden. They had gone but a few miles, when, to their astonishment, they encountered the advanced guard of the American army. The two forces were thus comparatively but a short distance apart, and this distance was rapidly diminishing. Linlower took his place in the ranks, while the Spy passed on is order to see the commander. When presented, the General expressed some displeasure at his prolonged absence; but, when he received his information, and learned what perils his faithful servant had undergone for him, he shook him by the hand and thanked him again and again.

"You see, Gineral," said the Spy, feeling perfectly at ease, "they've chose a purty bad piece of ground for us, but I don't think them Injins will fight as they used to. Howsumever, I s'pose it's best to be ready for 'em."

"Very true, my good friend; and I suppose you wish to bear a hand in the coming battle, do you not?"

"You're right there, Gineral; if I can only meet Tecumseh face to face, one or both of us will be wiped out."

"I understand there is a particular grudge between you and him. I suppose you have no objections to letting so good a friend as I into your secret. But, your rifle is gone. You must have one, certainly."

This abrupt turn of the conversation was kindly made by the General, the instant he witnessed the embarrassment and confusion of his humble friend. He forbore to press a question which he saw occasioned so much pain to the recipient.

"Yes, I shall need one. Ah's me! It'll be a hard job to supply the place of Spitfire; but I think I can manage to use another with some effect upon the red villains."

"You shall have it; and let me present you with this pistol, hoping you will make good use of it, as I am sure you will."

"No fear of that—no fear of that, Gineral," replied the Spy receiving the pistol with a low bow. The weapon was a beautifully ornamented one, and the honest fellow did not conceal the pleasure he experienced in accepting it. He was qualified to use it.

"And now, my friend, where do you wish to take your position? What company do you wish to join?"

"Them!" replied the Spy, pointing to the left.

"Those? They are Colonel Johnson's mounted regiment. You shall be a member in twenty minutes, however."

And twenty minutes later, the Forest Spy was mounted on a magnificent horse of a spotted color, and riding in line with this celebrated mounted regiment. In addition to this, he was also furnished with a military cap containing a red plume. It was indeed a valuable acquisition to the force. Many of the members recognized him as he came up, and their greetings were hearty and abundant.

The advanced guard of the American army moved forward Reaching the third unfordable tributary of the Thames, they found the bridge gone, and a large body of Indians drawn up to dispute the passage. Harrison, believing that the entire British forces were also present, formed in order of battle.

Two six-pounders were directed across the streams, and fired at the savages, who, after a few shots, withdrew and continued their retreat up the river. The truth was that Proctor, after selecting this ground, changed his mind. Leaving Tecumseh and a number of his men to defend the crossing, the Briton moved his main army further up, where he halted and made his dispositions for the final struggle. After making a show of resistance, the chief drew off his men and retreated, determined that he would no longer prevent Proctor from tasting the battle himself. Upon reaching the British troops, he halted and told his followers that the final stand was to be made. He took off his sword, and, handing it to a brother chief, said: "When my son becomes a distinguished warrior, and able to wield a sword, give this to him." He then removed his British military dress, and, clothed only as an ordinary warrior, took his position in line, remarking to the chiefs who were around him:

"My brother warriors! we are now about entering on an engagement *from which I shall never come out. My body will remain on the field of battle.*"

In a couple of hours the Americans had replaced the bridge, when the troops passed over. They followed on after the retreating army, and at the Moravian Towns found them disposed for battle. A few minutes' observation showed that their position was well chosen. Being on the northern side of the Thames, at a point unfordable, their left flank was thus protected, while their right extended some two hundred and fifty yards northward, through a swamp, in which Tecumseh, with nearly two thousand warriors, was stationed. This flank was thus amply guarded, while the left was additionally strengthened by the artillery, which was stationed in the road. The British troops were a few less in number than a thousand.

General Harrison, finding the wings of the enemy could not be turned, resolved to concentrate his forces against the British line. Accordingly, Trotter's brigade was drawn up in front of the enemy; one hundred yards behind this was stationed Chiles', and at the same distance in the rear of this was posted King's, as the reserve. The second division, consisting of two brigades, was formed at right angles to the first division. Simrall's regiment of light infantry was drawn up so as to cover the rear of the first division, their position being an oblique one in respect to the different brigades. A detachment of United States infantry took the intervening space between the road and river, for the purpose of making a demonstration against the enemy's artillery. The information of Forest Spy led General Harrison to adopt an ingenious accompaniment to this movement. It was arranged that forty friendly Indians should pass under the bank of the river, and, raising their war-cry in the rear of the enemy, make them believe their own Indians had turned against them. Governor Shelby, senior Major-General of the Kentucky troops, was at the head of five brigades numbering eighteen hundred men, and stationed between the first and second divisions. Johnson's mounted regiment was ordered to advance to the left as soon as the first division was in motion, and make an effort to turn the right flank of the Indians in the swamp. At the head of the army, of course, was General Harrison, with his staff, including Commodore Perry and General Cass.

Just as the orders were about to be issued for the first line to advance, Colonel Wood approached Harrison, and announced the curious fact that the British line was drawn up in *open order* instead of the usual compact or close order.

"I will make a novel movement, then," said the General, with animation. "Drawn up in that fashion, their regulars can not withstand a vigorous charge, and we will see what Colonel Johnson's regiment can do for them."

Harrison advanced to the right of the front column of mounted troops, led by a brother of Colonel Richard M. Johnson, and gave the orders himself. He directed him to charge at full speed upon the enemy, well satisfied that he could accomplish all that was desired. As soon as the preparations were completed, the regiment charged directly toward the British line at a tremendous pace. A heavy fire was poured into them, and the front column recoiled; but it was only momentary. They burst forward and came down upon the enemy with irresistible impetuosity, scattering the soldiers like leaves before the wind. The fire of the Indians being especially galling. Simrall's regiment hastened to the rescue, and the battle now became furious upon both sides. The swamp was like the repeated explosions of a mine, lit up with the incessant flashes of their rifles, and the belching smoke. The voice of Tecumseh, awful in its power, was heard above all, cheering on his men, and inciting their bravery to a point equal to his own. The rattle of the musketry, the booming of the cannon, the shouts of officers, the yells of Indians and men, made a scene that, for a few minutes, was indescribable.

When Johnson's regiment spurred away toward the Indian lines, (Colonel *James Johnson* charged the British lines, his brother charged Tecumseh's,) Forest Spy was carried away by the thrilling excitement of the moment Uttering a regular Creek war-cry, he thundered forward, and, in a few moments was engaged in one of the fiercest battles of his life. In the midst of the horrid din he heard the pealing voice of Tecumseh, rising like the blast of a trumpet. Carried forward by his mettled charger, he suddenly found himself near the chief, who was engaged in a deadly struggle with Gorman Lindower. The latter had made a thrust at his antagonist with a bayonet, but Tecumseh, catching it in his left hand, held it there, and was raising his tomahawk to brain him.

"Hold! here is your enemy," shouted the Spy, pressing toward the combatants. The chieftain, turning a look of concentrated hate upon his new foe, and still retaining the bayonet, drew back his tomahawk for the purpose of hurling it at him, when the Forest Spy discharged his pistol, and Tecumseh fell dead at his feet.*

The silence of Tecumseh was instantly noticed, and the words "He has fallen!" passed with electrical swiftness among his followers. The British lines had been irrecoverably broken, and their officers saw that the day was already lost. Not the least remarkable fact connected with the battle of the Thames was its brevity. While it lasted it raged with the most deadly fury, and it ceased almost as suddenly as it commenced. The British surrendered, and the remaining Indians fled. Among those who resorted to flight was the British General, Proctor, himself. He was hotly pursued by Colonels Chambers, Woods, Todd, and three or four privates, among whom was Gorman Lindower. He succeeded in making good his escape, but his baggage was captured. In his portfolio was found a translation of the speech of Tecumseh given in the preceding chapter.

After the battle the Forest Spy dismounted and was walking over the ground, when he noticed an old man, arrayed as a hunter, engaged in earnest conversation with a middle-aged and handsome Colonel. Both were on foot, and so intent with each other's words, that they noticed no one besides themselves. Something in the appearance of the hunter struck the Spy as familiar. He paused, and minutely examined his countenance. Suddenly his face lighted up, and stepping forward, he placed his hand on the hunter's shoulder, and said:

"I beg pardon, my friend; but I believe I have met you before. Do you know me?"

The Colonel paused and looked in his face, while the old hunter let his eye fall from the Spy's head to his feet, and then raised them from his feet to his head again.

* I saw Tecumseh engaged in a personal rencounter with a soldier armed with a musket; the latter made a thrust at the chief, who caught the bayonet under his arm, where he held it, and was in the act of striking his opponent with his tomahawk, when a horseman rode up, and shot Tecumseh dead with a pistol. The horseman had a red feather (plume) in his hat, and was mounted on a spotted or red-roan horse. I saw Tecumseh's body several days after the battle and it was not mutilated.—*Statement of Chambles, a Pottawatomie chief, to Captain Robert Anderson of the United States Army.*

"Do you make me out?"

The hunter shook his head.

"Are you Dick Dingle?"

The hunter nodded.

"And you," said the Spy, turning toward the Colonel, "are Russell Mansfield?"

"Right, sir; there is something about you that seems like an old acquaintance, but I am as much at a loss to tell as friend Dick Dingle here."

"Look close, both of you," said the Spy with a laugh; "I am an old acquaintance, and one you had no idea of meeting in this place."

The two scrutinized his countenance, but an expression of perplexity on their own showed the failure of their attempt to recognize him.

"Dick Dingle," said the Spy, compressing his lips together, and laying his hand upon his shoulder, "I've hunted for years with you and you don't remember me; and you, Colonel Mansfield, you once knew me; but it was many years ago, and time, I suppose, has changed me as well as yourselves. Call to mind your own wife, how you gained her, think of Jim Peterson, of his wife, the Frontier Angel, and of Monowano the Spy, and then see whether you can place me. You can not, I see; then," removing his plumes, "behold before you Peter Jenkins."

"Freeze me to death! is that you, sure?" exclaimed Dingle, grasping his hand. "I thought you'd gone under, years ago."

"It is really Jenkins," added Colonel Mansfield, taking his hand in turn. "I can recognize him now; strange that he should have so changed in a few years. Your hair is actually sprinkled with gray, when it was perfectly black a dozen years ago. But, give an account of yourself, Jenkins. Why have you remained hid so long?"

"I haven't been hid, Colonel; you, I'll agree, have heard of me more than once. But as I must shortly go, I will explain matters now, being there is not much to explain. You recollect, Dingle, what a foolish part I took in the hunt for the Frontier Angel, in the Nickajack Expedition, and when we went a trail-hunting together. I was one of the biggest cowards that ever breathed; that's the fact. What is more, I didn't care, either, for it. But, when the trouble along the frontier was over, I made an effort to get a wife. I found everybody had heard of my doings, and the girls just laughed in my face. I went to a dozen, I guess; but it was no use. They had all heard of me, and I found that everybody despised me. As I had no parents or home, I was miserable. I never felt the disgrace of being a coward before, and it wasn't long before I despised myself more than any one else.

"I brooded thus for the whole winter that I stayed in your section. In the spring, you remember, I left without bidding any one good-by. I made a vow that I would never take up my own name again, or show my face in them parts till I had earned the name of being a *brave* man. I wandered about in the woods for two or three years, until, about five years ago, when I was in one of the settlements in the States, a fine military-looking man came and asked my name. I gave him one that I had adopted and have carried to this day. The sound of it pleased him and he questioned me as to what I had been doing. I told him I had served under Wayne and St. Clair, and many others, as scout, and recommended him to them if he wished to learn more regarding me—knowing at the same time that he'd never take the trouble. Well, we halted awhile, and at last he made me an offer to serve him as spy. The offer was a good one, and the office one that I wanted; so I accepted it and the agreement was finished. I found that my employer was no other than General Harrison himself. He told me Tecumseh was stirring up the Injins and there would soon be trouble. He wanted me to watch that chief's movements and report every thing suspicious to him. I told him I would do so, and for five years I have done hardly any thing else. I have tramped from the Great Lakes to the Gulf of Mexico, and camped on nearly every big river between them. I went through your settlement twice, and met Jim Peterson. I told him what I was doing, the name I went under, and made him agree to tell nobody till I give him leave. I followed Tecumseh like his shadow—in canoes, through the woods, north, south east, and west. I met him in disguise, slept within a dozen yards of him without his knowing it, listened to his speeches from tree-tops or from among his own men, have drawn knives with him, have been condemned to the stake by him, and to-day have made an end of matters by *shooting him!* Besides crossing him in so many things, I am about to triumph over him in another way, which I need not explain just now. And I believe I have won a name which I need not be ashamed of."

"And what is that, pray?" asked Mansfield, greatly interested.

"*The Forest Spy.*"

"Are you the Forest Spy? Indeed you have then. I have heard that name spoken by hundreds, and every one praised it. General Harrison, in my hearing, told his staff, that no man living had done better service."

"Did the General say that?" asked the Spy, his eyes filling with tears.

"Ay, and more. He said you should be rewarded, too, and whatever station of life he might be called upon to fill he would ever be proud to recognize you as one of his best friends."

"God bless the Gineral—God bless the Gineral," replied the Spy, drawing his sleeve across his eyes.

"You're a trump, freeze-me if you ain't!" exclaimed Dingle, slapping him on the back. "You've got a name that any chap might feel proud of. But, you ain't *married* yet?"

"Not quite, but I hope I soon shall be."

"Good for you, again! You'll go home with us, *in course*."

"Certainly, there are hundreds who will grasp you by the hand," added Mansfield.

"No; I can't at present; but I will soon visit you. Where do you live?"

"We both left the settlement some years ago, and moved to Cincinnati. Peterson has done the same. I live with my son who has *about* forty children. The Colonel, here, is raising a tremendous crop too. Come down and make a call, bring your wife along, and stay fifteen or twenty years. We'll talk over old times ag'in, freeze me if we won't. Hurry up and find your wife and come along!"

The tears were in the eyes of Dingle as he uttered these earnest words. Colonel Mansfield added, in a feeling voice:

"I join my wishes with friend Dingle; and, as you have promised, shall count upon seeing you in Cincinnati in a short time. Our recent victories, I feel confident, have ended the war, and a reign of peace has commenced. I trust, then, Cincinnati will be your permanent home."

"Very likely, if it *suits the family*."

"How soon do you leave?"

"In a half-hour at any rate. Another person goes with me."

"When may I expect you in Cincinnati?"

"In a week, and like enough sooner."

"Inquire for me first," said Dingle. "You'll find the latch string hanging out, and a welcome waiting you inside."

"I hear my name called," said Mansfield, hurriedly. "Good by, for the present."

The Forest Spy shook hands with both as they moved away. A few minutes later some one touched him on the shoulder. Lindower stood beside him.

"Well, what's wanting, Gorman?"

"I believe we are not wanted any more in these parts."

"Well, what of it?"

"Umph!"

"No; there's no 'umph!' about it. We must be off."

A few minutes later, the two left the battle-ground, and disappeared in the forest.

## CHAPTER X.

### CONCLUSION.

> Thus far with rough and all unable pen
> Our bending author hath pursued the story;
> In little room confining mighty men,
> Mangling by starts the full course of their glory.
> — KING HENRY V.

LINDOWER and the Spy walked forward through the forest for several miles without speaking; each had his own thoughts, and for the present desired to commune with them. The Spy was filled with that peculiar anxiety—that mingling of hope, fear and doubt, which agitates the lover when nearing the object of his love for the first time in a long period. He felt that the crisis of his fate was at hand. That Laura Lindower was safe, he was assured, but would he be able to recover her? Had he not failed before? True, Tecumseh, the greatest obstacle, was removed by death; but there were other enemies remaining. Should Nockwynee be dead, he felt indeed the case was about hopeless, for he had no friends among the Indians besides him, and to present himself in the camp, alone and unprotected, immediately after such a disastrous defeat, would be equivalent to inviting his own destruction.

The sun was just sinking beyond Lake St. Clair, as the two hunters halted upon a small eminence which overlooked the Indian village. Although still at a good distance, the dismal sounds of wailing and lamentation were plainly heard, and the squaws could be seen passing to and fro, beating their breasts, tearing their hair, and chanting in an impassioned monotone the praises and deeds of their husbands or brothers who had fallen in battle. The whole village was given over to the reign of woe.

"'Tis a sad sight," said the Spy, extending his hand toward the village, and turning toward his companion. "'Tis a sad sight, I was saying, Gorman, and one that makes me feel almost as womanish as them squaws that are bellowing yonder; but, 'twas their own fault. Their warriors went into the war, and they have shared the fortunes of war."

"Umph!"

"The battle of the Thames has made a hole in them tribes that'll be felt as long as an Injin lives; Tecumseh's idee—that of an 'Injin Confederacy,' as the Gineral called it, will never be heard ag'in.'

"Umph!"

"But the night is coming on, Gorman, and I won't deny I've a hankering to be in that village yonder, inquiring about Laura's health. This may be a risky undertaking for me, and it'll consequently be much worse for both of us. I don't want to influence your action, Gorman, not in the least; but I will say if I go into that hornet's nest, *I go alone.* I'm not going to have the care of you upon my mind. You must stay behind, that's settled. *You are not going with me;* still, Gorman, I don't wish to influence your ideas at all. Act as you think best."

"Umph! you fool; who intended to go with you."

"I know your judgment, Gorman. When you get a few years older, and have had summat more of experience, you'll make a decent hunter. You'll remain here then till I return."

Saying which, the Spy strode down the declivity and made his way toward the Indian village. Lindower watched his receding form until it had nearly reached its destination, when, with a muttered "Umph!" he shook his head, and walked down the opposite side of the hill, where he prepared himself to wait the return of his venturesome friend.

The Forest Spy made his way forward with great caution, for he was fully sensible of the danger incurred by a white man in approaching the savages, at such a time. When within a few rods of the encampment, he drew his blanket over his head, bowing himself forward, and walking with a slow, measured tread, as if stricken with grief and sorrow. He walked through the narrow street, apparently without raising his eyes, but in reality keeping a careful scrutiny on every side. He saw more than one dark eye fixed inquiringly upon him; but, nothing was said until he had reached a point near the center of the village, when a large, darkly-painted warrior stepped in front of him, and asked, in English:

"Whence comes my brother?"

"From beyond the lakes," replied the Spy, in the Shawnee tongue.

"What does he wish?" asked the savage, in the latter dialect.

"He seeks a friend."

"The red-men have fallen by the river yonder, and how knows my brother that his friend is still on his feet?"

"Is Nockwynee, the Creek, in the village?"

"He is in yon lodge, mourning the fall of Tecumseh, Wasegoboah and his brother warriors."

"I would see him. Will my red brother conduct me to him?"

The Indian motioned to the Spy to follow, and led the way for a short distance through the main street, when he paused before a lodge, which the hunter at once recognized by its make as Tecumseh's own. The Indian then stepped aside for him to enter. The Spy did so, with slow steps, and with the same air of dejection and sorrow. Within the lodge were Nockwynee and Laura Lindower. The former was chanting the great deeds of Tecumseh in that nasal, dreary monotone so characteristic of the Indian's grief! He glanced up as the visitor stepped inside, but continued his chant without any sign of recognition. Laura Lindower was sitting with hands folded, meekly listening to the demonstration of her companion. She started slightly as she saw the Spy, but her respect for Nockwynee held her quiet. She instantly let her eyes fall to the ground, and remained as mute and motionless as a statue.

For fully half an hour the Spy stood, with bowed head and sealed lips. Then, as the lamentations of Nockwynee ceased, instead of making his errand known, he commenced chanting a dirge over the death of the great Tecumseh. He recounted many of his exploits mentioned by Nockwynee, and when his stock was exhausted did not fail to draw freely upon his imagination for a supply. The body of the Shawnee leader nor any of his blood relatives being present, the Spy suspected the truth—that it had been mutilated and disgraced by some of the men in the American army. Of course, he refrained from making any reference to the absence of the body, but continued the dirge as though it were present.

When he had finished, he advanced toward Nockwynee, and speaking in the Creek dialect, offered his sympathy. He conversed in low, impressive tones for several minutes, without taking any more notice of Laura Lindower than he would were she absent. While still conversing, Nockwynee motioned for her to approach. She did so, full of trembling and doubt. The Creek chief then placed her hand in that of the Forest Spy, and signified for them to depart. In answer to her inquiring look, he said, in the Shawnee tongue:

"'Tis the wish of Tecumseh. He said he should fall in the battle, and told those who survived him to restore the White Lily to its stem."

Holding her hand, the Spy passed out of the lodge into the narrow street, and slowly made his way out of the village. Both walked with their heads bent—the Spy having his blanket drawn over his—and resembled a couple of culprits walking to their doom.

Down between the noisy, wailing mourners they passed with the same solemn steps, exchanging no words with any one, not even themselves—out into the open country—rod after rod, furlong after furlong, until they ascended the hill from which the Spy and Lindower had viewed the village together. As they reached the bottom, the Spy looked back and saw that they were now hid from the view of the savages. Dropping his blanket to the ground, he sprung fully six feet in the air, with an ear-splitting scream, and exclaimed:

"Whoop! hurrah! the battle's won, and the vow of Peter Jenkins is accomplished. I have won a name that will disgrace no man living, and, more than that, I have won a wife at last after hunting for one for nigh onto twenty years. Heigh, Gorman! where are you?"

"Umph!"

It was the exclamation of Gorman Lindower, as he pressed his long-lost sister to his breast.

"Come, say something more than 'Umph'" said the Spy, "for you've good reason to, and so have I."

"I think it's time we moved, then," said Lindower, relinquishing his sister.

"You're right there, Gorman."

The blood-red sun was just dipping into Lake St. Clair, as the three entered the forest and took the direction of the American camp. The way was comparatively easy and their weaker companion experienced no difficulty in keeping up quite a brisk walk. Conversing together, recounting experiences, and explaining questions, Gorman Lindower found that, most singularly enough, he had been ignorant of many of the following facts.

While a resident on the frontier, along the river, some years before, Tecumseh had visited his neighborhood. In fact, being a Shawnee, his real home was not far distant. Although a married and middle-aged man, the passions of his youth were still strong in his bosom. He accidentally encountered Laura Lindower one day, and Indian-like, asked her to accompany him to his Indian lodge. Of course she declined this honor; but as she knew the chief possessed the means of accomplishing his ends should he desire to do so, she endeavored to impart her refusal "tenderly." The result was the chieftain was encouraged; and, although at that time he was planning and consummating one of the greatest rebellions that had ever desolated our frontiers, still, he found time to harass the "White Lily," as he poetically named her. She sometimes hardly left the house, so great was her fear of meeting him; but, when she was compelled to venture forth, he was sure to spring up like some prowling panther. She refrained from telling her brother, knowing that he would commit some rash act—probably attempt to murder the chief. It was at this time that Peter Jenkins, under the name of the Forest Spy, made his appearance. After a time Laura made known her trouble to him, and asked his advice. He was sorely troubled how to act. He was willing (after due warning to the chief) to shoot him; but he well knew such a procedure would precipitate the whole West into a bloody war, as the followers of Tecumseh would avenge his death. His only proposal was for them to move further east, into the land of civilization, where she would be safe from his interference. Upon proposing this to Gorman Lindower, to their surprise he expressed a determination to emigrate *south*—into what was known as the *Creek* country. The Spy strenuously opposed this, knowing that in that remote land, the power of Tecumseh would be absolute. Lindower, as we have before remarked, was a man of but few words, but when he had formed a resolution, nothing could turn him from its execution. Finding he would go, the Spy directed him to a certain section, where he believed he was less likely to be disturbed. The brother and sister emigrated, and he lost all sight of them for two years. Though their removal was effected with the greatest possible care and secrecy, Tecumseh discovered their destination. In 1811, when he went south to stir up the southern tribes, he dispatched a number of Shawnees and Creeks to take the two prisoners. The duties of the Forest Spy, who may have been said to haunt Tecumseh, of course had led him in that direction likewise; and, in the beginning of this work, we have shown how he arrived upon the scene of action, but a few hours after the abduction was accomplished.

It must have been at this time that Tecumseh learned an American scout was ever dogging his footsteps, and that between him and his fair prisoner was a bond stronger than friendship. He used the most strenuous exertions to capture this daring Spy who thus crossed his path in more than one sense. In the preceding pages we have recorded but few of the traps and stratagems from which the wily fellow escaped. We have all read of great and ambitious men who were continually thwarted by some one, that seemed born to be in their way. Thus was it for several years with Tecumseh. Fate, Destiny, Providence, or whatever it may be termed, protected the Forest Spy, and even when in the hands of his mortal enemy, when the Spy had resigned all hope, he was delivered. Two objects animated the Spy—that of rescuing Laura Lindower, and that of baffling and defeating the realization of Tecumseh's ambitious dreams. And both of these were accomplished—the Spy adding a fitting climax to the latter triumph, by shooting the great chief.

Although Tecumseh was guilty of Laura's abduction, still, his subsequent conduct was in keeping with his chivalrous character. A few months after Laura Lindower's capture, she told him she could never consent to become the squaw of any

Indian, much less of one who, like himself, was already provided for. Although he still retained her as a prisoner, yet he never afterward referred to the matter. When she asked to be allowed to return to her people, he promised her that she should at the close of the war, and, as we have stated, before going into the battle of the Thames, he left positive instructions that her wishes should be complied with in every respect. In truth, it may be said, that she could not have been better provided for during those distracted times, had she been restored to her friends.

Our three friends spent the following night in the American camp, and accompanied the army on its triumphal return to the States. They remained a long time in Cincinnati, with their old acquaintances, or rather with the Spy's acquaintances. The reunion of Peterson, Dingle, Jenkins, Mansfield, and the various characters which have before figured upon the stage of action, was one of peculiar interest, and one that was cherished by all to their dying day.

---

As this is the last time the Forest Spy will ever be brought before our readers, the following scene will be looked upon with some interest by a portion at least of those who have followed him through so many and varied adventures:

On one of the many beautiful islands that are scattered like gems in the bosom of the Ohio, stands a small, humble cottage, buried in trees, shrubbery and flowers. Travelers, as they hurry by, on the magnificent steamers which ornament our western rivers, catch a glimpse of its white, neat-looking front, and a few years since they sometimes noticed an old man, with locks white as the driven snow, who often wandered up and down the islands with his rifle in hand. Now and then, when the circling flocks ventured too near, the report of his gun was heard, and the bird fluttering to the ground, told that though his eye was dimmed and his hand palsied by time, yet his aim was almost as dangerous as ever.

At the close of a summer day in 1840, this old man was sitting in his cottage-door, listening to his grandson, a bright boy of some eight or ten years, who was reading a Cincinnati paper. His head was bowed upon his cane, and his whole soul was absorbed in the words which he heard. A few feet distant was seated the gray-haired partner of his joys and sorrows, in the large family rocking-chair. She had laid aside her knitting, and was also listening, with folded hands, to the words of her grandson. A young woman was engaged in preparing the evening meal, occasionally glancing toward her father and mother, and admonishing her boy to read somewhat slower and more distinctly. Her husband, a man doing business in the "Queen City," had not yet returned, but was expected momentarily. Without, tumbling upon the grass, were several smaller children, too young and too much engaged to notice the troubles of older heads. The meal being ready, the wife seated herself and gave attention to the contents of the newspaper. The periodical was printed with a broad black border, and heavy column lines, and the boy was reading an account of the death of President Harrison. As he finished, the old man exclaimed:

"God bless the Gineral; he will go to heaven if anybody will! I know'd he'd be President some day, but I thought he'd live to stand it through, when he was elected. I left the service in 1813; he told me I should be rewarded, and I have been. This island, this home, every thing, you know, Laura, came through his hand. Didn't it do my soul good to shake the Gineral by the hand, when he went on to Washington to take his seat, and he wasn't no way backward either. I heard him tell them big men around him who I was, and then they shook hands with me too, and they said they were as glad as the Gineral to see me. God bless him!"

The old man paused, for his eyes were streaming with tears, and his wife was similarly affected.

"He was a good man," said she, "and has had a good man's reward."

"Every word true—every word true," added the old man, in a choking voice.

"Just such a man as I'm bound to be," said the youngster, springing to his feet, and commencing a song known in those days as "Old Tippecanoe."

At this moment a young, fine-looking man came laughing into the door, followed by the children, all shouting and chasing him, several of whom called him "father!" and whooped for him to stop and romp with them. As he entered, the others arose and took a seat around the board. A blessing was invoked by the old man—once the FOREST SPY—and soon all were discussing in subdued and feeling voices, the great affliction which the country had just suffered.

THE END.

# STANDARD
# DIME DIALOGUES
### For School Exhibitions and Home Entertainments.

Nos. 1 to 21 inclusive. 15 to 25 Popular Dialogues and Dramas in each book. Each volume 100 12mo pages, sent post-paid, on receipt of price, ten cents.

**Beadle & Adams, Publishers, 98 William St., N. Y.**

These volumes have been prepared with especial reference to their availability for Exhibitions, being adapted to schools and parlors with or without the furniture of a stage, and suited to SCHOLARS AND YOUNG PEOPLE of every age, both male and female. It is fair to assume that no other books in the market, at any price, contain so many useful and available dialogues and dramas of wit, pathos, humor and sentiment.

## DIME DIALOGUES, NO. 1.

Meeting of the Muses. For nine young ladies.
Baiting a Live Englishman. For three boys.
Tasso's Coronation. For male and female.
Fashion. For two ladies.
The Rehearsal. For six boys.
Which will you Choose? For two boys.
The Queen of May. For two little girls.
The Tea-Party. For four ladies.
Three Scenes in Wedded Life. Male and female.
Mrs. Snifles' Confession. For male and female.
The Mission of the Spirits. Five young ladies.
Hobnobbing. For five speakers.
The Secret of Success. For three speakers.
Young America. Three males and two females.
Josephine's Destiny. Four females, one male.
The Folly of the Duel. For three male speakers.
Dogmatism. For three male speakers.
The Ignorant Confounded. For two boys.
The Fast Young Man. For two males.
The Year's Reckoning. 12 females and 1 male.
The Village with One Gentleman. For eight females and one male.

## DIME DIALOGUES, NO. 2.

The Genius of Liberty. 2 males and 1 female.
Cinderella; or, The Little Glass Slipper.
Doing Good and Saying Bad. Several characters.
The Golden Rule. Two males and two females.
The Gift of the Fairy Queen. Several females.
Taken in and Done For. For two characters.
The Country Aunt's Visit to the City. For several characters.
The Two Romans. For two males.
Trying the Characters. For three males.
The Happy Family. For several 'animals.'
The Rainbow. For several characters.
How to Write 'Popular' Stories. Two males.
The New and the Old. For two males.
A Sensation at Last. For two males.
The Greenhorn. For two males.
The Three Men of Science. For four males.
The Old Lady's Will. For four males.
The Little Phil osophers. For two little girls.
How to Find an Heir. For five males.
The Virtues. For six young ladies.
A Connubial Eclogue.
The Public meeting. Five males and one female.
The English Traveler. For two males.

## DIME DIALOGUES, NO. 3.

The May Queen. For an entire school.
Dress Reform Convention. For ten females.
Keeping Bad Company. A Farce. For five males.
Courting Under Difficulties. 2 males, 1 female.
National Representatives. A Burlesque. 4 males.
Escaping the Draft. For numerous males.
The Genteel Cook. For two males.
Masterpiece. For two males and two females.
The Two Romans. For two males.
The Same, Second scene. For two males.
Showing the White Feather. 4 males, 1 female.
The Battle Call. A Recitative. For one male.

## DIME DIALOGUES, NO. 4.

The Frost King. For ten or more persons.
Starting in Life. Three males and two females.
Faith, Hope and Charity. For three little girls.
Darby and Joan. For two males and one female.
The Way. A Floral Fancy. For six little girls.
The Enchanted Princess. 2 males, several females.
Honor to Whom Honor is Due. 7 males, 1 female.
The Gentle Client. For several males, one female.
Phrenology. A Discussion. For twenty males.
The Stubbletown Volunteer. 2 males, 1 female.
A Scene from "Paul Pry." For four males.
The Charms. For three males and one female.
Bee, Clock and Broom. For three little girls.
The Right Way. A Colloquy. For two boys.
What the Ledger Says. For two males.
The Crimes of Dress. A Colloquy. For two boys.
The Reward of Benevolence. For four males.
The Letter. For two males.

## DIME DIALOGUES, NO. 5.

The Three Guesses. For school or parlor.
Sentiment. A "Three Person'd" Farce.
Behind the Curtain. For males and females.
The Eta Pi Society. Five boys and a teacher.
Examination Day. For several female characters.
Trading in "Traps." For several males.
The School Boys' Tribunal. For ten boys.
A Loose Tongue. Several males and females.
How Not to Get an Answer. For two females.
Putting on Airs. A Colloquy. For two males.
The Straight Mark. For several boys.
Two Ideas of Life. A Colloquy. For ten girls.
Extract from Marino Faliero.
Ma-try-Money. An Acting Charade.
The Six Virtues. For six young ladies.
The Irishman at Home. For two males.
Fashionable Requirements. For three girls.
A Bevy of I's (Eyes). For eight or less little girls.

## DIME DIALOGUES, NO. 6.

The Way They Kept a Secret. Male and females.
The Poet under Difficulties. For five males.
William Tell. For a whole school.
Woman's Rights. Seven females and two males.
All is not Gold that Glitters. Male and females.
The Generous Jew. For six males.
Shopping. For three males and one female.
The Two Counselors. For three males.
The Votaries of Folly. For a number of females.
Aunt Betsy's Beaux. Four females and two males.
The Libel Suit. For two females and one male.
Santa Claus. For a number of boys.
Christmas Fairies. For several little girls.
The Three Rings. For two males.

# Dime School Series—Dialogues.

## DIME DIALOGUES No. 7.

The two beggars. For fourteen females.
The earth-child in fairy-land. For girls.
Twenty years hence. Two females, one male.
The way to Windham. For two males.
Woman. A poetic passage in words. Two so...
The 'Olugists. A Colloquy. For two males.
How to get rid of a bore. For several boys.
Boarding-school. Two males and two females.
Plan for the pledge. For two males.
The ills of dram-drinking. For three boys.
True pride. A colloquy. For two females.
The two lecturers. For numerous males.

Two views of life. Colloquy. For two females.
The rights of music. For two females.
A hopeless case. A query in verse. Two girls.
The would-be school-teacher. For two males.
Come to life too soon. For three males.
Eight o'clock. For two little girls.
True dignity. A colloquy. For two boys.
Grief too expensive. For two males.
Hamlet and the ghost. For two persons.
Little red riding hood. For two females.
New application of an old rule. Boys and girls.
Colored cousins. A colloquy. For two males.

## DIME DIALOGUES No. 8.

The fairy School. For a number of girls.
The enrolling officer. Three girls and two boys.
The base ball enthusiast. For three boys.
The girl of the period. For three girls.
The fowl rebellion. Two males and one female.
Slow but sure. Several males and two females.
Candidie's velocipede. One male and one female.
The figures. For several small children.
The trial of Peter Sloper. For seven boys.

Getting a photograph. Males and females.
The society for general improvement. For girls.
A nobleman in disguise. Three girls and six boys.
Great expectations. For two boys.
Playing sick. Five females and four males.
Clothes for the heathen. One male, one female.
A hard case. For three boys.
Ghost. For two females and one male.

## DIME DIALOGUES No. 9.

Advertising for help. For a number of females.
America to England, greeting. For two boys.
The old and the new. Four females, one male.
Choice of trades. For twelve little boys.
The lap-dog. For two females.
The victim. For four females and one male.
The duelist. For two boys.
The true philosophy. For females and males.
A good education. For two females.

The law of human kindness. For two females.
Spoiled children. For a mixed school.
Brutus and Cassius.
Coriolanus and Aufidius.
The new scholar. For a number of girls.
The self-made man. For three males.
The May queen (No 2.) For a school.
Mrs. Lackland's economy. 4 boys and 2 girls.
Should women be given the ballot? For boys.

## DIME DIALOGUES No. 10.

Mrs. Mark Twain's shoe. One male, one female.
The old flag. School festival. For three boys.
The court of folly. For many girls.
Great lives. For six boys and six girls.
Scandal. For numerous males and females.
The light of love. For two boys.
The flower children. For twelve girls.
The deaf uncle. For three boys.
A discussion. For two boys.

The rehearsal. For a school.
The true way. For three boys and one girl.
A practical life lesson. For three girls.
The monk and the soldier. For two boys.
1776-1876. School festival. For two girls.
Lord Dundreary's Visit. 2 males and 2 females.
Witches in the cream. For 3 girls and 2 boys.
Frenchman. Charade. Numerous characters.

## DIME DIALOGUES No. 11.

Appearances are very deceitful. For six boys.
The conundrum family. For male and female.
Curing Betsy. Three males and four females.
Jack and the beanstalk. For five characters.
The way to do it and not to do it. 3 females.
How to become healthy, etc. Male and female.
The only true life. For two girls.
Classic colloquies. For two boys.
I. Gustavus Vasa an' Cristiern.
II. Tamerlane and Bajazet.

Fashionable dissipation. For two little girls.
A school charade. For two boys and ter (?)
Jean Ingelow's "Songs of Seven." Several.
A debate. For four boys.
Ragged Dick's lesson. For three boys.
School charade, with tableau.
A very questionable story. For two boys.
A colt. For three males.
The real gentleman. For two boys.

## DIME DIALOGUES NO. 12.

Yankee assurance. Forseveral characters.
Gardeners wanted. For several characters.
When I was young. For two girls.
The must predict a heritage. For two boys.
The double cure. Two males and four females.
The flower-garden fairies. For five little girls.
Jeannine's novel. Three males and two females.
Beware of the widows. For three girls.

A family not to pattern after. Two characters.
How to man-age. An acting charade.
The vacation escapade. Four boys and teacher.
That naughty boy. Three females and a male.
Mad-cap. An acting charade.
All is not gold that glitters. Acting proverb.
Sic transit gloria mundi. Acting charade.

## DIME DIALOGUES NO. 13.

Two o'clock in the morning. For three males.
An indignation meeting. For several females.
Before and behind the scenes. Several charact's.
The noblest boy. A number of boys and teacher.
Blue Beard. A dress piece. For girls and boys.
Not so bad as it seems. For several characters.
A curious moral. For two males and one female.
Taste vs. sentiment. For parlor and exhibition.

Worth, not wea lth. For four boys and a teacher.
No such word as fail. For several males.
The sleeping beauty. For a school.
An innocent intrigue. Two males and a female.
Old Nably, the fortune-teller. For three girls.
Boy-talk. For several little boys.
Mother is dead. For several little girls.
A practical illustration. For two boys and girl.

# Dime School Series—Dialogues

## DIME DIALOGUES No. 14.

Mrs. James Jones. Three gents and two ladies.
The born genius. For four gents.
More than one listener. For four gents and lady.
Who on earth is he? For three girls.
The right not to be a pauper. For two boys.
Woman nature will out. For a girls' school.
Bachelor and bachelor. For two boys.
The cost of a dress. For five persons.
The surprise party. For six little girls.
A practical demonstration. For three boys.

Reclamation. Acting charade. Several characters.
Conscience, the arbiter. For lady and gent.
How to make mothers happy. For two boys.
A conclusive argument. For two girls.
A woman's blindness. For three girls.
Rum's work (Temperance.) For four gents.
The fatal mistake. For two young ladies.
Eyes and nose. For one gent and one lady.
Retribution. For a number of boys.

## DIME DIALOGUES No. 15.

The fairies' escapade. Numerous characters.
Aunt Betsy's perplexities. For six gentlemen.
A house cure. For two ladies and one gent.
The good there is in each. A number of boys.
Gentlemen of monkey. For two boys.
The little philosopher. For two little girls.
Aunt Polly's lesson. For four ladies.
A wind-fall. Acting charade. For a number.
Will it pay? For two boys.

The heir-at-law. For numerous males.
Don't believe what you hear. For three ladies.
A safety rule. For three ladies.
The chief's resolve. Extract. For two males.
Testing her friends. For several characters.
The foreigner's troubles. For two ladies.
The cat without an owner. Several characters.
Natural selection. For three gentlemen.

## DIME DIALOGUES No. 16.

Polly Ann. For four ladies and one gentleman.
The meeting of the winds. For a school.
The good they did. For six ladies.
The boy who wins. For six gentlemen.
Good-by day. A colloquy. For three girls.
The sick well man. For three boys.
The investigating committee. For nine ladies.
A "corner" in rogues. For four boys.

The lump of the trunk room. For five girls.
The boosters. A Colloquy. For two little girls.
Kitty's funeral. For several little girls.
Stratagem. Charade. For several characters.
Testing her scholars. For numerous scholars.
The world is what we make it. Two girls.
The old and the new. For gentleman and lady.

## DIME DIALOGUES No. 17.

LITTLE FOLKS' SPEECHES AND DIALOGUES.

To be happy you must be good. For two little girls and one boy.
Evanescent glory. For a bevy of boys.
The little peacemaker. For two little girls.
What parts friends. For two little girls.
Martha Washington tea party. For five little girls in old-time costume.
The evil sheep is in it. For two young boys.
Wise and foolish little girl. For two girls.
A child's inquiries. For small child and teacher.
The cooking club. For two girls and others.
How to do it. For two boys.
A hundred years to come. For boy and girl.
Don't trust them. For several small boys.
Above the skies. For two small girls.
The true heroism. For three little boys.
Give us little boys a chance: The story of the plum pudding; I'll be a man; A little girl's rights speech; Johnny's opinion of grand-mothers; The boasting hen; He knows der rest; A small boy's view of corns; Robby's sermon; Nobody's child; Nothing at grandpa Gray's; Little boy's view of how Columbus discovered America; Little girl's view; Little boy's speech on time; A little boy's soliloquy; The midnight murder; Robby Rob's second sermon; How the baby came; A boy's observations; The new slate; A mother's love; The cowslip' glory; Baby Lu la; Jack Billings on the bumble-bee, wren, alligator; Died yesterday; The chicken's mistake; The hair apparent; Deliver us from evil; Don't want to be good; Only a drunken fellow; The two little robins; He show to condemn; A nonsense tale; Little boy's declamation; A child's desire; Sugar; The goblin cat; Rob a dab; Calumny; Little chatterbox; Where are they; A boy's view; The twenty frogs; Going to school; A morning bath; The girl of Dundee. A fancy; In the twilight; The new laid egg. The little musician; Idle Sam; Pottery-wise. Then and now.

## DIME DIALOGUES No. 18.

Fairy wishes. For several characters.
No rose without a thorn. 2 males and 1 female.
Too greedy by half. For three males.
One good turn deserves another. For 6 ladies.
Courting Melinda. For 2 boys and 1 lady.
The new scholar. For several boys.
The little intercessor. For four ladies.
Antecedents. For 3 gentlemen and 3 ladies.

Give a dog a bad name. For two gentlemen.
Spring-time wishes. For six little girls.
Last Charlie; or, the gypsy's revenge. For numerous characters.
A little tramp. For three little boys.
Hard times. For 2 gentlemen and 4 ladies.
Two lessons well worth learning. For two males and two females.

## DIME DIALOGUES, NO. 19.

An awful mystery. Two females and two males.
Contentment. For five little boys.
Who are the spirits? For three young girls.
California uncle. Three males and three females.
Be kind to the poor. A little folks' play.
How people are insured. A duett.
Mayor. Acting charade. For four characters.
The smoke fiend. For four boys.
A kindergarten dialogue. For a Christmas festival. Presented by seven characters.
The use of study. For three girls.

The refined simpletons. For four ladies.
Remember Benson. For three males.
Modern education. Three males and one female.
Mad with too much love. For three males.
The fairy's warning. Dress piece. For two girls.
Aunt Eunice's experiment. For several.
The mysterious G. C. Two females and one male.
We'll have to mortgage the farm. For one male and two females.
An old fashioned duet.
The auction. For numerous characters.

## Dime School Series—Speakers.

### DIME DIALECT SPEAKER, No. 24.

Dot's vot's de matter,
The Mississippi miracle,
Ven to bide Gunns in,
Dr. es tame vot Mary had,
Pat O'Flaherty on woman's rights,
The home rulers, how they "spakes,"
Hannibal Dawson on Mothers-in-law,
He didn't sell the farm
The true story of Franklin's kite,
Would I were a boy again,
A pathetic story,
All about a bee,
Scandal,
A dark side view,
To poesor vay,
On learning German,
Mary's shmall vite lamb
A healthy discussion,
For lies not to speak,
Ool Mrs. Grimes,
A parody,
Mare and colt,
Lill Underwood, pilot,
Ned Granley,
The pill peddler's oration,
Widder Green's last words,
Latest Chinese outrage,
The manifest destiny of the Irishman,
Peggy McCann,
Sprays from Josh Billings,
De circumstances ob de situwation,
Dar's nuffin new under de sun,
A Negro religious poem,
That violin,
Picnic delights,
Our candidate's views,
Demosreey's wind on,
Plain language by truthful Jane,
My neighbor's dogs,
Condensed Mythology,
Picton,
The Noveden,
Legends of Attica,
The short-pipe tragedy,
A debtor's doxology,
The coming man,
The illegant affair of Mulderer's,
That little baby in the corner,
A goose in a tree,
An invitation to the bird of liberty,
The crow,
Out west.

### DIME READINGS AND RECITATIONS, No. 24.

The Irishman's panorama,
The lightning-rod agent,
The tragedy at Iver cottage,
Ruth and Naomi,
Cato of Corson,
Ma bien,
J ha Reed,
The Irishman at church,
Parson Mooah's sermon at,
Arguing the question
Sim Webb and the cow,
The dim old forest,
Banker at home,
The Sergeant's story,
David and Goliah,
Dreaming at fourscore,
Rum,
Why should the spirit of mortal be proud?
The evening mustache,
The engineer's story,
A candidate for president,
Roll call,
An accession to the family,
When the cows come home,
The donation party,
Tommy Taft,
A Michigander in France,
Not one to spare,
Mrs. Bouncy's pink lunch,
Rock of ages,
J. Cæsar Pompey Squash's sermon,
Annie's ticket,
The newsboy,
Pat's correspondence,
Death of th' owd squire
Mons'eg Shmedd,
At Elberon,
The cry of womanhood,
The judgement day,
The heart bubble,
Curfew must not ring to-night,
The swell,
The water mill,
Sam's letter,
I'm tolope of the dead,
Charity,
An essay on church.

☞ The above books are sold by Newsdealers everywhere, or will be sent, post-paid, to any address, on receipt of price, 10 cents each.

**BEADLE AND ADAMS, Publishers, 98 William St., N. Y.**

# STANDARD BOOKS OF GAMES AND PASTIMES.

**BEADLE AND ADAMS, PUBLISHERS, NEW YORK.**

## HAND-BOOK of SUMMER ATHLETIC SPORTS.

CONTENTS:—Pedestrianism; Walkers vs. Runners; Scientific Walking (3 cuts); Scientific Running (2 cuts); Dress for Pedestrians; Training for a Match; Laying out a Track (1 cut); Conducting a Match; Records of Pedestrianism; Jumping and Pole-leaping (1 cut); Bicycling; Rules for Athletic Meetings; Hare and Hounds (1 cut); Archery (1 cut). Fully illustrated. By Capt. Fred. Whittaker.

## HAND-BOOK OF CROQUET.

A Complete Guide to the Principles and Practice of the Game. This popular pastime has, during the few years of its existence, rapidly outgrown the first vague and imperfect rules and regulations of its inventor; and, as almost every house at which it is played adopts a different code of laws, it becomes a difficult matter for a stranger to assimilate his play to that of other people. It is, therefore, highly desirable that one uniform system should be generally adopted, and hence the object of this work is to establish a recognized method of playing the game.

## DIME BOOK OF 100 GAMES.

Out-door and in-door SUMMER GAMES for Tourists and Families in the Country, Picnics, etc., comprising 100 Games, Forfeits and Conundrums for Childhood and Youth, Single and Married, Grave and Gay. A Pocket Hand-book for the Summer Season.

## CRICKET AND FOOT-BALL.

A desirable Cricketer's Companion, containing complete instructions in the elements of Bowling, Batting and Fielding; also the Revised Laws of the Game; Remarks on the Duties of Umpires; the Mary-le Bone Cricket Club Rules and Regulations; Bets, etc. By Henry Chadwick.

## HAND-BOOK OF PEDESTRIANISM.

Giving the Rules for Training and Practice in Walking, Running, Leaping, Vaulting, etc. Edited by Henry Chadwick.

## YACHTING AND ROWING.

This volume will be found very complete as a guide to the conduct of watercraft, and full of interesting information alike to the amateur and the novice. The chapter referring to the great rowing-match of the Oxford and Cambridge clubs on the Thames, will be found particularly interesting.

## RIDING AND DRIVING.

A sure guide to correct Horsemanship, with complete directions for the road and field; and a specific section of directions and information for female equestrians. Drawn largely from "Stonehenge's" fine manual, this volume will be found all that can be desired by those seeking to know all about the horse, and his management in harness and under the saddle.

## GUIDE TO SWIMMING.

Comprising Advisory Instructions; Rules upon Entering the Water; General Directions for Swimming; Diving; How to Come to the Surface; Swimming on the Back; How to Swim in times of Danger; Surf-bathing—How to Manage the Waves, the Tides, etc.; a Chapter for the Ladies; a Specimen Female Swimming School; How to Manage Cases of Drowning; Dr. Franklin's Code for Swimmers; etc. Illustrated. By Capt. Philip Peterson.

☞ For sale by all newsdealers; or sent, post-paid, to any address, on receipt of price—TEN CENTS each.

**BEADLE AND ADAMS, PUBLISHERS, 98 WILLIAM ST., N. Y.**

# BEADLE'S NEW DIME NOVELS.

| | | | |
|---|---|---|---|
| 378 Table, the Trailer. | 303 Red Slayer. | 446 The Two Hunters. | 509 The Rangers of the Mohawk. |
| 339 The Boy Chief. | 394 The Phantom Foe. | 449 The Traitor Spy. | |
| 340 Tim, the Trailer. | 395 Blue Anchor. | 450 The Gray Hunter. | 510 The Double Hand. |
| 341 Red Ax, the Giant. | 396 Kenchin's Pledge. | 451 Little Moccasin. | bad Alice Wilde. |
| 342 Nialla, the Spy. | 397 Quadroon Spy. | 452 The White Hermit. | 505 Ruth Margerie. |
| 343 White Avenger. | 398 Black Rover. | 453 The Island Bride. | 506 Privateer's Cruise. |
| 344 The Indian King. | 399 Red Belt. | 454 The Forest Princess. | 507 The Indian Queen. |
| 345 The Long Trail. | 400 The Two Trails. | 455 The Trail Hunters. | 508 The Wrecker's Prize. |
| 346 Kirk, the Guide. | 401 The Ice-Fiend. | 456 Backwoods Banditti. | 509 The Slave Sculptor. |
| 347 The Phantom Trail. | 402 The Red Prince. | 457 Ruby Roland. | 510 Backwoods Bride. |
| 348 The Apache Guide. | 403 The First Trail. | 458 Laughing Eyes. | 511 Chip, the Cave Child |
| 349 The Mad Miner. | 404 Sheet-Anchor Tom. | 459 Mahaska, Maiden. | 512 Bill Biddon, Trapper |
| 350 Keen-eye, Ranger. | 405 Old Avoirdupois. | 460 The Quaker Scout. | 513 Cedar Swamp. |
| 351 Blue Belt, Guide. | 406 White Gladiator. | 461 Brother's Scouts. | 514 |
| 352 On the Trail. | 407 Blue Clipper. | 462 The Two Champions. | |
| 353 The Specter Spy. | 408 Red Dan. | 463 The Two Guards. | |
| 354 Old Bald-head. | 409 The Fire-Eater. | 464 Quindaro. | 517 Gray Jack, the Guide |
| 355 Red Knife, Chief. | 410 Blackhawk. | 465 Rob Roskin. | 518 Off and On. |
| 356 Sib Cone, Trapper. | 411 The Lost Ship. | 466 The Rival Rovers. | 519 Seth Jones. |
| 357 The Bear-Hunter. | 412 Black Arrow. | 467 Ned Starling. | 520 Emerald Necklace. |
| 358 Bashful Bill, Spy. | 413 White Sergeant. | 468 Single Hand. | 521 Malaeska. |
| 359 The White Chief. | 414 The Lost Captain. | 469 Tippy, the Texan. | 527 Burt Bunker. |
| 360 Cortina, the Scourge | 415 The Twin Trailors. | 470 Young Mustanger. | 523 Pale Face Squaw. |
| 361 The Squaw Spy. | 416 Death's Head Ranger | 471 The Hunted Life. | 524 Winifred Winthrop. |
| 362 Scout of '76. | 417 Captain of Captains. | 472 The Buffalo Trapper. | 525 Wrecker's Daughter. |
| 363 Spanish Jack. | 418 Warrior Princess. | 473 Old Zip. | 526 Hearts Forever. |
| 364 Masked Spy. | 419 The Blue Band. | 474 Foghorn Phil. | 527 The Frontier Angel |
| 365 Kirk, the Renegade. | 420 The Squaw Chief. | 475 Mustaseet, the Brave. | 528 Florida. |
| 366 Dingle, the Outlaw. | 421 The Flying Scout. | 476 Snow-Bird. | 529 The Maid of Esopus. |
| 367 The Green Ranger. | 422 Sonora Bev. | 477 Dragoon's Bride. | 530 Ahmo's Plot. |
| 368 Megibara, Scourge. | 423 The Sea King. | 478 Old Honesty. | 531 The Water Waif. |
| 369 Metamora. | 424 Mountain Old. | 479 Bald Eagle. | 532 The Hunter's Cabin. |
| 370 Thornpath, Trailer. | 425 Death-Trailer. | 480 Black Princess. | 533 Hates and Loves. |
| 371 Foul-weather Jack. | 426 The Crested Serpent. | 481 The White Brave. | 534 Oonomoo, the Huron. |
| 372 The Black Rider. | 427 Arkansas Kit. | 482 The Riflemen of the Miami. | 535 White-Faced Pawn. |
| 373 The Helpless Hand. | 428 The Corsair Prince. | | 536 Wetzel, the Scout. |
| 374 The Lake Rangers. | 429 Eben Allen's Ride. | 483 The Moose Hunter. | 537 The Quakeress Spy. |
| 375 Alone on the Plains. | 430 Little Thunderbolt. | 484 The Brigantine. | 538 Valley Scout. |
| 376 Phantom Horseman. | 431 The Falcon Rover. | 485 Put Pomfret's Ward. | 539 Uncle Ezekiel. |
| 377 Winona. | 432 Honest Hand. | 486 Simple Phil. | 540 Westward Bound. |
| 378 Silent Shot. | 433 The Stone Chief. | 487 Jo Davies's Client. | 541 Wild Raven. |
| 379 The Phantom Ship. | 434 The Gold Demon. | 488 Ruth Harland. | 542 Agnes Falkland. |
| 380 The Red Rider | 435 Eatawan, Slaver. | 489 The Gulch Miners. | 543 Nathan Todd. |
| 381 Grizzly-Hunters. | 436 The Masked Guide. | 490 Captain Molly. | 544 Myrtle, the Child of the Prairie. |
| 382 The Mad Ranger. | 437 The Conspirators. | 491 Wigwagwad. | |
| 383 The Specter Skipper. | 438 Selfwing, Squaw. | 492 The Fearless Spy. | 545 Lightning Jo. |
| 384 The Red Coyote. | 439 Caribou Zip. | 493 The Peon Prince. | 546 The Blacksmith of Antwerp. |
| 385 The Hunchback. | 440 The Privateer. | 494 The Sea Captain. | |
| 386 The Black Wizard. | 441 The Black Spy. | 495 Graybeard. | 547 Madge Wylde. |
| 387 The Mad Horseman. | 442 The Doomed Hunter. | 496 The Border Rivals. | 548 The Creole Sisters. |
| 388 Privateer's Bride. | 443 Barden, the Ranger. | 497 The Unknown. | 549 Star Eyes. |
| 389 Jaguar Queen. | 444 The Gray Scalp. | 498 Sagamore of Saco. | 550 Myra, the Child of Adoption. |
| 390 Shadow Jack. | 445 The Peddler Spy. | 499 The King's Man. | |
| 391 Eagle Plume. | 446 The White Canoe. | 500 Adam and Ashore. | 551 Hawkeye Harry. |
| 392 Ocean Outlaw. | 447 Eph Peters. | 501 The Wrong Man. | |

The following will be issued in the order and on the dates indicated:

552 **Dead Shot.** By Albert W. Aiken. Ready September 24th.
553 **The Boy Miners.** By Edward S. Ellis. Ready October 8th.
554 **Blue Dick.** By Captain Mayne Reid. Ready October 22d.
555 **Nat Wolfe.** By Mrs. M. V. Victor. Ready November 5th.
556 **The White Tracker.** By the author of "The Boy Miners." Ready November 19th.
557 **The Outlaw's Wife.** By Mrs. Ann S. Stephens. Ready December 3d.
558 **The Tall Trapper.** By Albert W. Aiken. Ready December 17th.
559 **The Island Pirate.** By Captain Mayne Reid. Ready January 1st.
560 **The Boy Ranger.** By Oll Coomes. Ready January 14th.
561 **Bess, the Trapper.** By Lieutenant J. H. Randolph. Ready January 28th.
562 **The French Spy.** By W. J. Hamilton. Ready February 11th.
563 **Long Shot.** By Captain Comstock. Ready February 25th.
564 **The Gunmaker of the Border.** By James L. Bowen. Ready March 11th.
565 **Red Hand.** By A. G. Piper. Ready March 25th.
566 **Ben, the Trapper.** By Major Lewis W. Carson. Ready April 8th.
567 **The Specter Chief.** By Seelin Robins. Ready April 22d.

Published semi-monthly. For sale by all newsdealers; or sent, post-paid, single numbers, ten cents; six months (13 Nos.) $1.25; one year (26 Nos.) $2.50.

**BEADLE AND ADAMS, Publishers, 98 William St., N. Y.**

New Series, No. 195. | Old Series No. 516.

# BEADLE'S
# NEW DIME NOVELS

## The Forest Spy.

# Popular Dime Hand-Books.

### BEADLE AND ADAMS, PUBLISHERS, NEW YORK.

*Each volume 100 12mo. pages, sent post-paid on receipt of price—ten cents each.*

## STANDARD SCHOOL SERIES.

**DIME SPEAKERS.**
1. Dime American Speaker.
2. Dime National Speaker.
3. Dime Patriotic Speaker.
4. Dime Comic Speaker.
5. Dime Elocutionist.
6. Dime Humorous Speaker.
7. Dime Standard Speaker.
8. Dime Stump Speaker.
9. Dime Juvenile Speaker.
10. Dime Spread eagle Speaker.
11. Dime Debater and Chairman's Guide.
12. Dime Exhibition Speaker.
13. Dime School Speaker.
14. Dime Ludicrous Speaker.
15. Carl Pretzel's Komikal Speaker.
16. Dime Youth's Speaker.
17. Dime Eloquent Speaker.
18. Dime Hail Columbia Speaker.
19. Dime Serio-Comic Speaker.
20. Dime Select Speaker.

Dime Melodist. (Music and Words.)
School Melodist. (Music and Words.)

**DIME DIALOGUES.**
Dime Dialogues Number One.
Dime Dialogues Number Two.
Dime Dialogues Number Three.
Dime Dialogues Number Four.
Dime Dialogues Number Five.
Dime Dialogues Number Six.
Dime Dialogues Number Seven.
Dime Dialogues Number Eight.
Dime Dialogues Number Nine.
Dime Dialogues Number Ten.
Dime Dialogues Number Eleven.
Dime Dialogues Number Twelve.
Dime Dialogues Number Thirteen.
Dime Dialogues Number Fourteen.
Dime Dialogues Number Fifteen.
Dime Dialogues Number Sixteen.
Dime Dialogues Number Seventeen.
Dime Dialogues Number Eighteen.
Dime Dialogues Number Nineteen.
Dime Dialogues Number Twenty.
Dime Dialogues Number Twenty-one.

## YOUNG PEOPLE'S SERIES.

1—DIME GENTS' LETTER-WRITER—Embracing Forms, Models, Suggestions and Rules for the use of all classes, on all occasions.
2—DIME BOOK OF ETIQUETTE—For Ladies and Gentlemen: being a Guide to True Gentility and Good-Breeding, and a Directory to the Usages of society.
3—DIME BOOK OF VERSES—Comprising Verses for Valentines, Mottoes, Couplets, St. Valentine Verses, Bridal and Marriage Verses, Verses of Love, etc.
4—DIME BOOK OF DREAMS—Their Romance and Mystery; with a complete Interpreting Dictionary. Compiled from the most accredited sources.
5—DIME FORTUNE-TELLER—Comprising the art of Fortune-Telling, how to read Character, etc.
6—DIME LADIES' LETTER-WRITER—Giving the various forms of Letters of School Days, Love and Friendship, of Society, etc.
7—DIME LOVERS' CASKET—A Treatise and Guide to Friendship, Love, Courtship and Marriage. Embracing also a complete Floral Dictionary, etc.
8—DIME BALL-ROOM COMPANION—And Guide to Dancing. Giving rules of Etiquette, hints on Private Parties, toilettes for the Ball-room, etc.
9—BOOK OF 100 GAMES—Out-door and In-door SUMMER GAMES for Tourists and Families in the Country, Picnics, etc., comprising 100 Games, Forfeits, etc.
10—DIME CHESS INSTRUCTOR—A complete hand-book of instruction, giving the entertaining mysteries of this most interesting and fascinating of games.
11—DIME BOOK OF CROQUET—A complete guide to the game, with the latest rules, diagrams, Croquet Dictionary, Parlor Croquet, etc.
12—DIME BOOK OF BEAUTY—A delightful book, full of interesting information. It deserves a place in the hands of every one who would be beautiful.

DIME ROBINSON CRUSOE—In large octavo, double columns, illustrated.

## FAMILY SERIES.

1. DIME COOK BOOK.
2. DIME RECIPE BOOK.
3. DIME HOUSEWIFE'S MANUAL.
4. DIME FAMILY PHYSICIAN.
5. DIME DRESSMAKING AND MILLINERY.

☞ The above books are sold by Newsdealers everywhere, or will be sent, postpaid, to any address, on receipt of price, 10 cents each. BEADLE & ADAMS Publishers, 98 William Street, New York.

# THE

# FOREST SPY.

## A TALE OF THE WAR OF 1812.

BY EDWARD S. ELLIS,
AUTHOR OF THE FOLLOWING DIME NOVELS:

332 RIVAL HUNTERS.
345 THE LONG TRAIL.
347 THE PHANTOM TRAIL.
348 THE APACHE GUIDE.
352 ON THE TRAIL.
376 PHANTOM HORSEMAN.
455 THE TRAIL HUNTERS.
460 THE QUAKER SCOUT.
502 RANGERS OF THE MOHAWK.
512 BILL BIDDON.

NEW YORK:
**BEADLE AND ADAMS, PUBLISHERS,**
98 WILLIAM STREET.

# STANDARD DIME DIALOGUES

### For School Exhibitions and Home Entertainments.

Nos. 1 to 21 inclusive. 15 to 25 Popular Dialogues and Dramas in each book. Each volume 100 12mo pages, sent post-paid, on receipt of price, ten cents.

**Beadle & Adams, Publishers, 98 William St., N. Y.**

These volumes have been prepared with especial reference to their availability for Exhibitions, being adapted to schools and parlors with or without the furniture of a stage, and suited to SCHOLARS AND YOUNG PEOPLE of every age, both male and female. It is fair to assume that no other books in the market, at any price, contain so many useful and available dialogues and dramas of wit, pathos, humor and sentiment.

## DIME DIALOGUES, NO. 1.

| | |
|---|---|
| Meeting of the Muses. For nine young ladies. | Hobnobbing. For five speakers. |
| Baiting a Live Englishman. For three boys. | The Secret of Success. For three speakers. |
| Tasso's Coronation. For male and female. | Young America. Three males and two females. |
| Fashion. For two ladies. | Josephine's Destiny. Four females, one male. |
| The Rehearsal. For six boys. | The Folly of the Duel. For three male speakers. |
| Which will you Choose? For two boys. | Dogmatism. For three male speakers. |
| The Queen of May. For two little girls. | The Ignorant Confounded. For two boys. |
| The Tea-Party. For four ladies. | The Fast Young Man. For two males. |
| Three Scenes in Wedded Life. Male and female. | The Year's Reckoning. 12 females and 1 male. |
| Mrs. Snifles' Confession. For male and female. | The Village with One Gentleman. For eight females and one male. |
| The Mission of the Spirits. Five young ladies. | |

## DIME DIALOGUES, NO. 2.

| | |
|---|---|
| The Genius of Liberty. 2 males and 1 female. | How to Write 'Popular' Stories. Two males. |
| Cinderella; or, The Little Glass Slipper. | The New and the Old. For two males. |
| Doing Good and Saying Bad. Several characters. | A Sensation at Last. For two males. |
| The Golden Rule. Two males and two females. | The Greenhorn. For two males. |
| The Gift of the Fairy Queen. Several females. | The Three Men of Science. For four males. |
| Taken in and Done For. For two characters. | The Old Lady's Will. For four males. |
| The Country Aunt's Visit to the City. For several characters. | The Little Philosophers. For two little girls. |
| The Two Romans. For two males. | How to Find an Heir. For five males. |
| Trying the Characters. For three males. | The Virtues. For six young ladies. |
| The Happy Family. For several 'animals.' | A Connubial Eclogue. |
| The Rainbow. For several characters. | The Public meeting. Five males and one female. |
| | The English Traveler. For two males. |

## DIME DIALOGUES, NO. 3.

| | |
|---|---|
| The May Queen. For an entire school. | The Genteel Cook. For two males. |
| Dress Reform Convention. For ten females. | Masterpiece. For two males and two females. |
| Keeping Bad Company. A Farce. For five males. | The Two Romans. For two males. |
| Courting Under Difficulties. 2 males, 1 female. | The Same. Second scene. For two males. |
| National Representatives. A Burlesque. 4 males. | Showing the White Feather. 4 males, 1 female. |
| Escaping the Draft. For numerous males. | The Battle Call. A Recitative. For one male. |

## DIME DIALOGUES, NO. 4.

| | |
|---|---|
| The Frost King. For ten or more persons. | The Stubbletown Volunteer. 2 males, 1 female. |
| Starting in Life. Three males and two females. | A Scene from "Paul Pry." For four males. |
| Faith, Hope and Charity. For three little girls. | The Charms. For three males and one female. |
| Darby and Joan. For two males and one female. | Bee, Clock and Broom. For three little girls. |
| The May. A Floral Fancy. For six little girls. | The Right Way. A Colloquy. For two boys. |
| The Enchanted Princess. 2 males, several females. | What the Ledger Says. For two males. |
| Honor to Whom Honor is Due. 7 males, 1 female. | The Crimes of Dress. A Colloquy. For two boys. |
| The Gentle Client. For several males, one female. | The Reward of Benevolence. For four males. |
| Phrenology. A Discussion. For twenty males. | The Letter. For two males. |

## DIME DIALOGUES, NO. 5.

| | |
|---|---|
| The Three Guesses. For school or parlor. | Putting on Airs. A Colloquy. For two males. |
| Sentiment. A "Three Persons'" Farce. | The Straight Mark. For several boys. |
| Behind the Curtain. For males and females. | Two Ideas of Life. A Colloquy. For ten girls. |
| The Eta Pi Society. Five boys and a teacher. | Extract from Marino Faliero. |
| Examination Day. For several female characters. | Ma-try-Money. An Acting Charade. |
| Trading in "Traps." For several males. | The Six Virtues. For six young ladies. |
| The School Boys' Tribunal. For ten boys. | The Irishman at Home. For two males. |
| A Loose Tongue. Several males and females. | Fashionable Requirements. For three girls. |
| How Not to Get an Answer. For two females. | A Bevy of I's (Eyes). For eight or less little girls. |

## DIME DIALOGUES, NO. 6.

| | |
|---|---|
| The Way They Kept a Secret. Male and females. | The Two Counselors. For three males. |
| The Poet under Difficulties. For five males. | The Votaries of Folly. For a number of females. |
| William Tell. For a whole school. | Aunt Betsy's Beaux. Four females and two males. |
| Woman's Rights. Seven females and two males. | The Libel Suit. For two females and one male. |
| All is not Gold that Glitters. Male and female. | Santa Claus. For a number of boys. |
| The Generous Jew. For six males. | Christmas Fairies. For several little girls. |
| Shopping. For three males and one female. | The Three Rings. For two males. |

## Dime School Series—Dialogues.

### DIME DIALOGUES No. 7.

The two beggars. For fourteen females.
The earth-child in fairy-land. For girls.
Twenty years hence. Two females, one male.
The way to Windham. For two males.
Woman. A poetic passage at words. Two mc
The Circulus. A Colloquy. For two males.
How to get rid of a bore. For several boys.
Boarding school. Two males and two females.
Fun for the pledge. For five males.
The ills of dram-drinking. For three boys.
True pride. A colloquy. For two females.
The two lecturers. For numerous males.

Two views of life. Colloquy. For two families.
The rights of music. For two women.
A hopeless case. A query in verse. Two girls.
The would-be schoolteacher. For two males.
Come to life too soon. For three males.
Eight o'clock. For two little girls.
True dignity. A colloquy. For two boys.
Grief too expensive. For two males.
Hamlet and the ghost. For two persons.
Little red riding hood. For two females.
New application of an old rule. Boys and girls.
Colored cousins. A colloquy. For two males.

### DIME DIALOGUES No. 8.

The fairy school. For a number of girls.
The enrolling officer. Three girls and two boys.
The base ball enthusiast. For three boys.
The girl of the period. For three girls.
The fowl rebellion. Two males and one female.
Slow but sure. Several males and two females.
Candida's visit. One male and one female.
The figures. For several small children.
The trial of Peter Slapem. For seven boys.

Getting a photograph. Males and females.
The society for general improvement. For girls.
A nobleman in disguise. Three girls, six boys.
Great expectations. For two boys.
Playing school. Five females and four males.
Clothes for the heathen. One male, one female.
A bad case. For three boys.
Ghost. For two females and one male.

### DIME DIALOGUES No. 9.

Advertising for help. For a number of females.
America to England, greeting. For two boys.
The old and the new. Forty females, no males.
Choice of trades. For twelve little boys.
The lap-dog. For two females.
The victim. For four females and one male.
The duelist. For two boys.
The dum photograph. For females and males.
A good education. For two females.

The law of human kindness. For two females.
Spoiled children. For a mixed school.
Brutus and Cassius.
Coriolanus and Aufidius.
The new scholar. For a number of girls.
The cold-made men. For three males.
The May queen (No. 2.) For a school.
Mrs. Lackland's economy. 4 boys and 3 girls.
Should women be given the ballot? For boys.

### DIME DIALOGUES No. 10.

Mrs. Mark Twitchy's visit. One male, one female.
The old district school festival. For three boys.
The sundry of after. For many girls.
Candid lives. For six boys and six girls.
Grandad. For numerous males and one female.
The light of love. For two boys.
The figure children. For twelve girls.
The deaf uncle. For three boys.
A dissolution. For two boys.

The rehearsal. For a school.
The only way. For three boys and one girl.
A practical life lesson. For three girls.
The myth and the soldier. For two boys.
1776-1876. School festival. For two girls.
Lord Dundreary's Visit. 3 males and 1 female.
Witches in the cream. For 3 girls and 4 boys.
Frenchman. Charade. Numerous characters.

### DIME DIALOGUES No. 11.

Appearances are very deceitful. For six boys.
The conundrum family. For male and female.
Curious Baby. Three males and four females.
Jack and the beanstalk. For five characters.
The way to do it and not do it. Females.
How to become healthy, etc. Male and female.
The only true life. For two girls.
Classic colloquies. For two boys.
I. Gustavus Vasa and Cristiern.
II. Tamerlane and Bazazet.

Fashionable dissipation. For two little girls.
A school charade. For two boys and two girls.
Jean Ingelow's "Songs of Seven." For 7 girls.
A debate. For four boys.
Ragged Dick's lesson. For three boys.
School charade, with tableau.
A very questionable story. For two boys.
A nail. For three males.
The real gentleman. For two boys.

### DIME DIALOGUES NO. 12.

Yankee assurance. Several characters.
Boarders wanted. For several characters.
When I was young. For two girls.
The most precious heritage. For two boys.
The double cure. Two males and four females.
The flower-garden fairies. For five little girls.
Jemima's novel. Three males and two females.
Beware of the widows. For three girls.

A family not to pattern after. Ten characters.
How to manage. An actable charade.
The vacation crusade. Four boys and teacher.
The naughty boy. Three females and a male.
Mad-cap. An acting charade.
All is not gold that glitters. Acting proverb.
Sic transit gloria mundi. Acting charade.

### DIME DIALOGUES NO. 13.

Two o'clock in the morning. For three males.
An indignation meeting. For several females.
Before and behind the scenes. Several character's.
The noblest boy. A number of boys and teacher.
Blue Beard. A dress piece. For girls and boys.
Not so bad as it seems. For several characters.
A connubial eclogue. For two males and female.
Scenes at the lyceum. For parlor and exhibition.

Worth, not worth. For four boys and a teacher.
No such word as fail. For several males.
The sleeping beauty. For a school.
An innocent intrigue. Two males and a female.
Old Nabbly, the fortune-teller. For three girls.
Boy-talk. For several little boys.
Mother is dead. For several little girls.
A practical illustration. For two boys and girl.

## Dime School Series—Dialogues

### DIME DIALOGUES No. 14.

Mrs. Jonas Jones. Three girls and two ladies.
The boy genius. For four genus.
Meet him as Linkum. For four gents and lady.
Who on earth is he? For three girls.
The right not to be a pauper. For two boys.
Woman nature will out. For a girls' school.
Benedict and bachelor. For two boys.
The cost of a dress. For five persons.
The surprise party. For six little girls.
A practical demonstration. For three boys.
Refinement. Acting charade. Several characters.
Conscience, the arbiter. For lady and gent.
How to make mothers happy. For two boys.
A conclusive argument. For two girls.
A woman's blindness. For three girls.
Rum's work (Temperance.) For four gents.
The fatal mistake. For two young ladies.
Eyes and nose. For one gent and one lady.
Retribution. For a number of boys.

### DIME DIALOGUES No. 15.

The fairies' escapade. Numerous characters.
A poet's perplexities. For six gentlemen.
A home cure. For two ladies and one gent.
The good there is in each. A number of boys.
Gentlemen or monkey. For two boys.
The little philosopher. For two little girls.
Aunt Polly's lesson. For four ladies.
A wind-fall. Acting charade. For a number.
Will it pay? For two boys.
The heir-at-law. For numerous males.
Don't believe what you hear. For three ladies.
A sad mistake. For three ladies.
The chief's resolve. Extract. For two males.
Testing her friends. For several characters.
The newsgirl's victory. For two ladies.
The cat without an owner. Several characters.
Natural selection. For three gentlemen.

### DIME DIALOGUES No. 16.

Polly Ann. For four ladies and one gentleman.
The meeting of the winds. For a school.
The good they did. For six ladies.
The boy who wins. For six gentlemen.
Good-by day. A colloquy. For three girls.
The sick well man. For three boys.
The investigating committee. For nine ladies.
A "corner" in argues. For four boys.
The imps of the trunk room. For five girls.
The bookman. A Colloquy. For two little girls.
Kitty's funeral. For several little girls.
Stratagem. Charade. For several characters.
Testing her scholars. For numerous scholars.
The world is what we make it. Two girls.
The old and the new. For gentlemen and lady.

### DIME DIALOGUES No. 17.

LITTLE FOLKS' SPEECHES AND DIALOGUES.

To be happy you must be good. For two little girls and one boy.
Evanescent glory. For a bevy of boys.
The little peacemaker. For two little girls.
What parts friends. For two little girls.
Martha Washington tea party. For five little girls in old-time costume.
The evil there is in it. For two young boys.
Wise and foolish little girl. For two girls.
A child's inquiries. For small child and teacher.
The cooking club. For two girls and others.
How to do it. For two boys.
A hundred years to come. For boy and girl.
Don't trust them. For several small boys.
Above the skies. For two small girls.
The true heroism. For three little boys.
Give us little boys a chance; The story of the plum pudding; I'll be a man; A little girl's rights speech; Johnny's opinion of grandmothers; The benefiting hen; He knows doesn't; A small boy's view of corns; Robby's sermon; Nobody's child; Nutting at grandpa Gray's; Little boy's view of how Columbus discovered America; Little girl's view; Little boy's speech on time; A little boy's pocket; The midnight murder; Robby Rob's second sermon; Here the baby came; A boy's observations; The new slate; A mother's love; The cowswain' glory; Baby Lou; Josh Billings on the bumble-bee, wren, alligator; Died yesterday; The chicken's mistake; The heir apparent; Deliver us from evil; I don't want to be good; Only a drunken fellow; The two little robins; He show to condemn; A newsman's tale; Little boy's declamation; A child's desire; Bogus; The public cat; Rubadub; Calomay; Little chatterbox; Where are they; A boy's view; The twenty frogs; Going to school; A morning bath; The girl of Dundee; A fancy; In the sunlight; The new laid egg; The little musician; Lite Bess Pottery-man; Then and now.

### DIME DIALOGUES No. 18.

Fairy wishes. For several characters.
No rose without a thorn. 2 males and 1 female.
Too greedy by half. For three males.
One good turn deserves another. For 6 ladies.
Courting Malinda. For 2 boys and 1 lady.
The new scholar. For several boys.
The little intercessor. For four ladies.
Antecedents. For 3 gentlemen and 3 ladies.
Give a dog a bad name. For two gentlemen.
Spring-time wishes. For six little girls.
Lost Charlie; or, the gipsy's revenge. For numerous characters.
A little tramp. For three little boys.
Hard times. For 2 gentlemen and 4 ladies.
The lesson well worth learning. For two males and two females.

### DIME DIALOGUES, NO. 19.

An awful mystery. Two females and two males.
Contentment. For five little boys.
Who are the saints? For three young girls.
California uncle. Three males and three females.
Be kind to the poor. A little folks' play.
How people are insured. A "duet."
Mayor. Acting charade. For four characters.
The smoke fiend. For five boys.
A kindergarten dialogue. For a Christmas Festival. Personated by seven characters.
The cup of doubt. For three girls.
The refined simpletons. For four ladies.
Remember Benson. For three males.
Modern education. Three males and one female.
Mad with too much lore. For three males.
The fairy's warning. Dress piece. For two girls.
Aunt Eunice's experiment. For several.
The mysterious G. G. Two females and one male.
We'll have to mortgage the farm. For one male and two females.
An old fashioned duet.
The auction. For numerous characters.

Dime School Series—Speakers.

## DIME DIALECT SPEAKER, No. 24.

Dat's wat's de matter,
The Mississippi miracle,
You're in tide cummin in,
Dicus fumes out Mary had
 a—,
Pat O'Flaherty on wo-
 man's rights,
The house raisers, how
 they "spakes,"
Hannibal Dawson at
 Mother's-in-law,
He didn't sell the farm,
The true story of Frank-
 lin's kite,
Would I were a boy
 again,
A pathetic story,

All about a bee,
Scandal,
A dark side view,
Topsey say,
On learning German,
Mary's almost vite lamb,
A healthy discourse,
How to learn to speak,
Old Mrs. Grimes,
A parody,
More sad cats,
Bill Underwood, pilot,
Old Granley,
The pill peddler's ora-
 tion,
Wilder Green's last
 words,

Latest Chinese outrage,
The manifest destiny of
 the Irishman,
Peggy McCann,
Sayings from Josh Bil-
 lings,
De circumstances ob d
 situation,
Dar's nuffin new under
 de sun,
A Negro religious poem,
That's so,
Picnic delights,
Our candidate's views,
Dundreary's wisdom,
Plain language by truth-
 ful James,

My neighbor's dog,
Condensed Mythology,
Pietro,
The Nereides,
Legends of Attica,
The stove-pipe tragedy,
A dubster's druthers,
The evening man,
The elegant affair of
 Muldoon's,
That little baby in
 the corner,
A genee the lair,
An invitation to the
 bird of liberty,
The crow,
Out went.

## DIME READINGS AND RECITATIONS, No. 24.

Two Irishman's pano-
 rama,
The lightning-rod agent,
The tragedy at bar asa
 flat,
Ruth and Naomi,
Caesar of Cerros,
Babies,
John Reed,
The brakeman at
 church,
Parson Mooah's ser-
 mon II,
Arguing the question,
Sam Wolfe and the cats,

The dim old forest,
Rupert at home,
The Sargeant's story,
David and Goliah,
Drowning at Lucknow,
Rum,
Why should the spirit
 of mortal be proud?
The rushing mustache,
The engineer's story,
A candidate for presi-
 dent,
Roll call,
An accession to the
 family,

When the cows come
 home,
The donation party,
Tommy Taft,
A Michigander in
 France,
Not one to spare,
Mrs. Browny's pink
 lunch,
Such of ages,
J. Caesar Pompey
 Squash's sermon,
Annie's ticket,
The cowboy,
Pat's correspondence,

Death of th' reed squire,
Mein tag Shroud,
At Elberon,
The cry of womanhood,
The judgment day,
The burst bubble,
Curfew must not ring
 to-night,
The swell,
The water mill,
Sam's letter,
Footsteps of the dead,
Charity,
An essay on cheek.

☞ The above books are sold by Newsdealers everywhere, or will be sent, post-paid, to any
 address, on receipt of price, 10 cents each.

**BEADLE AND ADAMS, Publishers, 98 William St., N. Y.**

# STANDARD BOOKS OF GAMES AND PASTIMES.

**BEADLE AND ADAMS, PUBLISHERS, NEW YORK.**

## HAND-BOOK of SUMMER ATHLETIC SPORTS.

Contents:—Pedestrianism; Walkers vs. Runners; Scientific Walking (3 cuts); Scientific Running (2 cuts); Dress for Pedestrians; Training for a Match; Laying out a Track (1 cut); Conducting a Match; Records of Pedestrianism; Jumping and Pole-leaping (1 cut); Bicycling; Rules for Athletic Meetings; Hare and Hounds (1 cut); Archery (1 cut). Fully illustrated. By Capt. Fred. Whittaker.

## HAND-BOOK OF CROQUET.

A Complete Guide to the Principles and Practice of the Game. This popular pastime has, during the few years of its existence, rapidly outgrown the first vague and imperfect rules and regulations of its inventor; and, as almost every house at which it is played adopts a different code of laws, it becomes a difficult matter for a stranger to assimilate his play to that of other people. It is, therefore, highly desirable that one uniform system should be generally adopted, and hence the object of this work is to establish a recognized method of playing the game.

## DIME BOOK OF 100 GAMES.

Out-door and in-door SUMMER GAMES for Tourists and Families in the Country, Picnics, etc., comprising 100 Games, Forfeits and Conundrums for Childhood and Youth, Single and Married, Grave and Gay. A Pocket Hand-book for the Summer Season.

## CRICKET AND FOOT-BALL.

A desirable Cricketer's Companion, containing complete instructions in the elements of Bowling, Batting and Fielding; also the Revised Laws of the Game; Remarks on the Duties of Umpires; the Mary-le-Bone Cricket Club Rules and Regulations; Bets, etc. By Henry Chadwick.

## HAND-BOOK OF PEDESTRIANISM.

Giving the Rules for Training and Practice in Walking, Running, Leaping, Vaulting, etc. Edited by Henry Chadwick.

## YACHTING AND ROWING.

This volume will be found very complete as a guide to the conduct of watercraft, and full of interesting information alike to the amateur and the novice. The chapter referring to the great rowing-match of the Oxford and Cambridge clubs on the Thames, will be found particularly interesting.

## RIDING AND DRIVING.

A sure guide to correct Horsemanship, with complete directions for the road and field; and a specific section of directions and information for female equestrians. Drawn largely from "Stonehenge's" fine manual, this volume will be found all that can be desired by those seeking to know all about the horse, and his management in harness and under the saddle.

## GUIDE TO SWIMMING.

Comprising Advisory Instructions; Rules upon Entering the Water; General Directions for Swimming; Diving; How to Come to the Surface; Swimming on the Back; How to Swim in times of Danger; Surf-bathing—How to Manage the Waves, the Tides, etc.; a Chapter for the Ladies; a Specimen Female Swimming School; How to Manage Cases of Drowning; Dr. Franklin's Code for Swimmers; etc. Illustrated. By Capt. Philip Peterson.

☞ For sale by all newsdealers; or sent, post-paid, to any address, on receipt of price—TEN CENTS each.

**BEADLE AND ADAMS, PUBLISHERS, 98 WILLIAM ST., N. Y.**

www.ingramcontent.com/pod-product-compliance
Lightning Source LLC
Chambersburg PA
CBHW020152170426
43199CB00010B/1005